All Together Now

Also by John Harvey Jones

Making it Happen
Getting it Together
Managing to Survive

JOHN HARVEY JONES

All Together Now

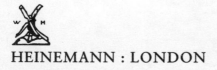

HEINEMANN : LONDON

First published in Great Britain 1994
by William Heinemann Ltd
an imprint of Reed Consumer Books Ltd
Michelin House, 81 Fulham Road, London SW3 6RB
and Auckland, Melbourne, Singapore and Toronto

Reprinted 1994

A CIP catalogue record for this book
is available at the British Library
ISBN 0 434 00228 3

Phototypeset by Intype, London
Printed in Great Britain by Clays Ltd, St Ives plc

*For Ferdie – my closest
friend, whose example thirty-seven
years ago led me to seek
a career as a manager.*

Contents

ONE The Conductor's Role

There is practically no area of business where the difference between rhetoric and actuality is greater than in the handling of people. Every businessman will always claim that it is the people in his organisation who are the key to its success. Indeed it is difficult to argue anything else. A company consists of money (which can ebb and flow almost with the speed of light), of fixed investments (which by definition are obsolescent from the very moment that they have been made), and a range of products – and hopefully a market position – which are under continual attack from competitors who are trying to produce better and more desirable products for less cost. What a company does have, and handled rightly can maintain, is the commitment, skills and abilities of its people. This is constantly attested to by the statements in company annual reports – I cannot remember the last time I failed to see the chairman's last sentence paying tribute to his people. Yet despite all these facts our skills at enabling our people to give their best, and continuously beat the best that come against them, are remarkably tenuous. Moreover, this area of activity is seldom subject to

1

the sort of analysis, debate and experimentation so readily devoted to fields such as production or marketing. Even though we are all wedded to the concept of continuous improvement, when did you last see an improvement plan for the management of your people? If you have seen one, I would bet long money that the plan referred to reduction of administration costs or overheads, rather than being a plan consciously adopted to enable more of our people to contribute more.

The problem is made even more difficult because we have no way of measuring how much better the whole outfit could do, let alone how much more each individual could contribute. Long ago work-study officers introduced the concept of 'rating' to address the rate at which people performed physical tasks, such as loading machines, opening valves or carrying out inspections, against a theoretical average. No such system exists to address, even in subjective terms, the rate of actual performance of people against their potential. The system does not exist for the very good reason that neither we nor they have any idea what that potential is. Each time we tell ourselves we have reached the limit we find we can go the extra mile. The fact that we do not have the tools to measure this gap does not, however, excuse us from making the effort. It is extraordinary that we are prepared to put more effort into improving our accountancy than into motivating our people. It is even odder that we would not expect a manager to manage any technical activity without exhaustive training, testing and coaching, while we assume that any technically qualified individual can be put in charge of people and produce results.

During this decade many of the sources of competitive advantage on which companies have traditionally been able to rely are being eroded. There was a time when a technological lead gave one a substantial, sustainable advantage against the competition, but today, with information technology, the newest and the best is almost instantly available across the world. The speed of modern communications and the force of international competition require the quickest possible adoption of new ideas if companies are to survive at all. Failure, not just to keep abreast of the best but to keep ahead of them, is rewarded by instantaneous eclipse. Nor is size any longer a guarantee of competitive advantage or longevity. Few would have credited that companies such as General Motors and IBM, which appeared impregnable, would be facing the traumas all three are involved in today.

Business is becoming more and more akin to intellectual sumo wrestling. Business success is based ever more directly and speedily on the abilities of the people in the business to change, foresee trends, take acceptable risks, be more in tune with tomorrow's needs of today's customers and to set their stalls out for the myriad economic and social changes which are occurring. To seize advantage in these ways is not a matter of brute force, but one of finely honed intelligence, coupled with genuine qualities of character and a continuous dedication to staying ahead in the race. Just as athletics demonstrate continuously that it is the frame of mind of the

3

athlete, rather than sheer physical power, which is the decisive factor in winning, so it is with business. But the difficulty is that, while few will contest these statements, few also follow the logic of their beliefs through to a coherent and consistent philosophy which imbues their company from top to bottom. Nor will you find these issues the subject of endless board debate and introspection. Even companies which have a clearly expressed and understood company style to which they attribute their competitive advantage have often come to it more by accident than by planning. Grand Metropolitan, with whom I have worked for many years, is proud of its 'restless' style of management, which is never satisfied with its achievements. But this characteristic, the reality of which I can attest, derives at least as much from the character of the chief executive as it does from deep philosophical debate.

It is true that, stimulated by books such as Tom Peter's *In Search of Excellence*, companies now consider it almost essential to have a 'mission' statement and a statement of values as well as, in some cases, a statement of ethical beliefs. Most of these statements show more sign of careful drafting by groups of people than of deeply held emotional belief. The suggestion that a company should re-examine its attitudes and beliefs about its people as a key measure to competitive success provokes a reaction rather like that of the little man in the H. M. Bateman cartoon. Companies are embarrassed, but in addition the majority of those in business do not actually know how to discuss or analyse their attitudes to people and how to harness their potential. All too often such a discussion changes into a debate about organisation, as though drawing lines on an organisation chart could alone change peoples' behaviour.

Recent years have seen the emergence of almost unbelievable dogma about the ways in which competitive business behaviour can be engendered in individuals. The most prominent of these is, I suppose, the belief that the unbridled and unfettered use of market forces will, on their own, ensure that people will give their best so that long-term effectiveness will ensue. The fear of unemployment, balanced by performance-related rewards, are thought to be enough in themselves to enlist whole-hearted commitment to excelling. The credo seems to be that men and women are motivated solely by economic considerations, and selfish ones at that, although I doubt that any reader of this book would recognise such behaviour in themselves. Indeed, fear of being fired is more likely to provoke a reaction of keeping one's head down and avoiding risk than a determination to succeed at a difficult task. All modern business is a matter of working with other people, both those within one's own company and outside suppliers and customers. Working with others calls for continual adjustment to their views and is a far more subtle pressure on the individual than sheer economics. The job of businessmen and women is to win – to create, lead, inspire and motivate teams of people who, by their creativity, speed of reaction, dedication and relevance to the needs of tomorrow, will ensure that their business gets in front and stays there.

There is increasingly a view that managing people is a

science. At least one prominent academic attributes the failures of British management to our inability to view management scientifically. I spent the largest part of my managerial life in a science-based industry, a company, moreover, which had a well justified belief in the scientific approach. However, the essence of science is reproducibility. I suggest that anyone who has worked with groups of people would readily agree that people react to stimuli quite randomly. One has only to take a moment to examine one's own reactions to external events to see how much they are coloured by emotional and other considerations which dominate our lives and our thinking. We do not react predictably, like a substance in a chemical experiment. The same group of people will react to the same events differently on Monday than on Friday. On Monday the week lies ahead of them and they are looking ahead to what they want to accomplish. On Friday many will already be thinking of the weekend delights with their family. Moreover, on Monday their home circumstances may be totally different from those on Friday. On Friday, Joe may be worried about his wife's illness which started on Thursday evening, or Harry may be concerned about an argument with his girlfriend, or Sue may be deeply anxious about her child's forthcoming exam. All these factors affect the way we react to the instructions, exhortations or managerial decisions we are given in the workplace.

In my view, management is not so much a science as an art. It is an art because management consists of enlisting the freely given support of disparate groups of people at different times to achieve, by their own free will, an agreed common purpose. The protagonists of scientific management receive my entire support when they plead that we should examine the facts behind management and managerial decisions more rigorously and attempt to learn from our previous experiences. But that is a far, far cry from claiming that people handled in particular ways will react predictably.

There has also been an ever more prevalent belief that in some way the logarithmic expansion of information technology and computing power will supersede the human brain, and reduce the human input into business. It is certainly true that these capabilities rendered unnecessary many of the routine tasks which have been done by human beings, but we blind ourselves if we think that business is going to be a computer chess game between our program and those of our rival company. Business is not a circumscribed operation. There are no defined rules, moves or actions, nor does it take place upon a prescribed stage. The essence of business is the almost total freedom which exists for any company or business to change itself in any way that the people involved wish it to. Far from replacing the human element in business, the growth of information technology places an even higher premium upon human skills. Even if it were possible to draw up computer programs to take ethical or market decisions, somebody would still have to define the limits of such decisions. I have made extensive use of market research in my business career, but anybody who believes that market research will always produce the right answer is failing to face facts. Some of the world's most successful products have been launched despite dire predictions of failure by the experts and scientific study of the potential demand for a product. It is well known that the Sony Walkman, one of the world's greatest successes, which created an entire new range of consumer products, was introduced by Morita, the boss of Sony, not only in defiance of market research but also of the views of his own managers. After all, by definition, people are unlikely to know that they need a product which does not exist, and the basis of market research in new and innovative products is limited in this regard.

Currently two completely contradictory views of the importance and role of people in business appear to be holding sway. The first is that only an elite minority of super-brains will be able to cope with the business demands of the future. The difficulty with this argument is that business is not just a question of logic and intelligence. Business is a battle of minds and wills. It calls for most extensive use of every human quality – be it courage, optimism, balance, judgement, humour, moral conviction, ethical values, sensitivity and so on. Unfortunately, from my own experience, the distribution of these human qualities does not equate with Mensa ratings of human intelligence. All of us are aware of the cliché of the absent-minded professor and the fact that men and women of breathtaking intellectual capability are often lacking in commonsense or the ability to deal with fellow human beings. Quite a surprising number of outstanding businessmen have been unsuccessful academically; neither Richard Branson nor Alan Sugar would claim to have achieved academic greatness, but few would argue with their impressive achievements as businessmen. Moreover, most business decisions are already far beyond the capability of single minds and single individuals. Business decision-making is increasingly a collective operation in which the ability to play as a team member, to listen, to build on the ideas of others and to make two and two equal five rather than three and a half which is the key to success.

There is little doubt in my mind that tomorrow's business scene requires the potential abilities of every man and woman, more particularly in Britain since we seem to find it so difficult to develop the capability of our people, except under conditions of war. While the idea of a vast unemployable group of people, depending for their well-being upon the success of a small elite group, is taking hold, there is a growing reductionist tendency to look upon people simply as 'human resources'. I am by nature a mild-mannered man who likes to consider himself tolerant and understanding; however, when people are referred to as 'human resources' and are evaluated in the same way as money, raw materials or technology, a red haze settles over my eyes. People are not a resource, they are people – in their glory, variety and ability. The problem is that not only do we undervalue our existing potential, but that we do so little to grow and develop our people. Since retiring from ICI, I have met larger numbers and a wider range of business people at every level than I did during my years with that company. I invariably challenge every company I visit by asking them what proportion of the capability of their people they think they are using. I have yet to meet a single one claiming that they are using as much as a half of their people's capabilities if they were released. We talk continuously about the need to improve our productivity and, God knows, it is a dire need; yet we appear to accept with equanimity that in the world of work we are achieving less than half of our capacity. Luckily for us, few other countries do much better, but the potential for improvement is so vast that it is incomprehensible that we do not debate, study and struggle to do better.

If you believe, as I do, that people are the true potential area for the revival of British business, you tend to be looked upon as a crank or a hopeless optimist. Nevertheless, as I have travelled around I have been impressed by the success of those who have tried to set their businesses and organisations on new paths by releasing the energy, capability, creativity and enthusiasm of their people. A certain amount of lip service has been paid, and a whole new business jargon, containing terms such as 'empowerment' and so on, has come into being, but it still seems impossible to discuss publicly the practical things which people can do to effect these changes. Personnel management has been increasingly aligned with administration; indeed, in this country management is considered synonymous, according to the Oxford Dictionary, with administration, control, organisation and regulation. The negative aspects of management, particularly with regard to people, are continuously harped upon – but the concept of a totally different and broader approach to the involvement of people in businesses of every size still seems as far away as ever it was. I find this all the more astonishing because everyone in this country has had personal, practical and sad experience of being managed badly at some time. We recognise when it is being done wrongly, we blossom on the rare occasions when it is done right, but we seem to accept that there is an inevitability about management and its attitudes to people about which we can do nothing. The difference between an organisation that was deeply concerned with the management of its people and one that was not was well exemplified by the contrast between shopping at Marks & Spencer and shopping at Woolworths before their sweeping management changes. The attitudes of the sales people, their commitment to their companies and their concerns for the customers spoke volumes for the pay off from concern for people. At the same time, on the rare occasions when a gifted manager (such as head teacher Bob Salisbury of the Garibaldi School in Mansfield, who has totally transformed a school operating within all the constraints that the British educational system imposes) manages to achieve something truly remarkable, this appears to be ascribed to some gift from God rather than to the sheer hard work, dedication and conviction involved.

The whole concept of management in Britain has been debased by being seen as synonymous with control and regulation. Control and regulation might be needed if every person in the country were madly enthusiastic and besotted by the desire for business success. Then they might need holding back to control the pace of change and advance. A more illusory picture of the business scene in the United Kingdom would be difficult to draw. We simply have to find (as I pointed out in my first management book *Making it*

Happen) ways of switching people on, rather than ways of turning people off. Of course management involves some elements of administration, of control and of calculation of risk, but these areas of managerial activities have been studied to death. Far too little has been written about how we address the creation of a better and more dynamic tomorrow. I believe that part of the reason for this overkill is that it is easy to measure the cost of administration, which is always looked upon as being an 'overhead', and an undesirable one at that. This leads to uniformity of treatment and determined efforts to force human behaviour into a rigid pattern of conformity, to reduce administrative costs to the minimum. It is assumed that all men and women are not only equal but similar in their reactions to incentives, rewards, punishment, exaltation and so on. How is it possible that sane and ordinary human beings, who glory in the differences of people's approaches, views, values, expectations and aspirations, can attempt to deal with the richness of the human tapestry in such prosaic 'cost effective' terms? The problem is that it is extremely difficult to produce a savings statement which compares a team operating at full speed, working flexibly, valuing each person's differences, building and creating, with the administration of the payment grading system, the promotions system or organisational hierarchy. Working as a team means flexibility of treatment and people always give their best when they believe they are valued as individuals. Nobody wants to be the same as anyone else. We all start with different basic ideas and it is weaving these ideas together into a dynamic whole which makes for the successful team.

There can be few organisations where the hierarchy and the reward systems are more rigid than they are in the services, where I spent the first twenty years of my working life. However, if you look at the way in which Special Air Service teams are organised and how they operate you can see that hierarchy is forgotten and team roles are given to those who are most suited to carry them out, irrespective of rank. Decisions are taken together as groups and there is a full understanding that what wins is the ownership of the plan, rather than slave-like adherence to somebody else's ideas. In business we seem to be as far away from these ideas as we can possibly get, despite the fact that anyone in any company knows that the way the company operates in theory bears little or no relation to the way in which it operates in reality. I believe that the companies which get the most out of their people are those whose values are consistent or, at minimum, harmonious with each other. This consistency is even more crucial because all of us who work with other people form our views of the sort of behaviour which is desirable from a host of different clues. In large organisations these clues come from many different people. The advertisement we respond to when seeking a job is written by one person, the interviewing and selection done by another. The administration is frequently done by people other than those to whom we directly respond. Almost everything in modern business is done by groups of people and each member of the group will probably display different behaviour and ideas about what is important to them. The reward system is seldom constructed to stimulate the behaviour that the group wishes to encourage, and most companies are clearer about what they do not want than what they do. Risk-taking is usually punished, as are deviations from the normal 'behaviour' of the group. All of this gives very different messages to people who are attempting to work together and contribute to the common goal.

One of the reasons why small organisations find it easier to release the energy and harness the capability of their people, thus becoming faster moving, more flexible and quicker to change than their larger counterparts, is because each employee comes into contact with fewer people and there is thus less conflict of message. Larger organisations have inbuilt characteristics which make it difficult for them to adjust quickly or make the best use of their people's capabilities.

Firstly, large organisations have been built on rigid hierarchical models which of themselves make team working difficult. Team working needs the involvement of people at every level. The practical consequences of managerial decisions are often known at the bottom of the hierarchy, and these people are difficult to involve if they are submerged by layers of supervisors, each of whom acts as a filter, adjusting the message to what they think their superiors will listen to. The Japanese involvement of their shop-floor people in continuous improvement *Kaizen* systems and their insistence on single status dress, canteens and so on are all attempts to overcome these hierarchical rigidities.

Secondly, large organisations are all too often character-ised by a cacophony of different messages and apparent aims. These occur even within businesses which have created a single selected value system – and those are in a minority. Stripping out layers of management and organising in differ-ent ways can ease these problems. Ultimately the businesses that win are those where all the people have the same aim and give freely in their commitment to it. Thirdly, large organisations seek harmony. They are concerned at the nega-tive effects of conflict and friction and so tend to suppress pressures for change. Of course too much conflict means that a business goes nowhere, but some friction is essential for movement and change. Large organisations have so many buffers between decisions and results that it is difficult to engender passion. Passivity is seen as a virtue instead of a danger. I am a fervent believer in the small unit, close to the customer, quick to react and able to function with some autonomy as a team. The dangers of a team working as a small unit are, however, that risk-taking may be discouraged. We rely on the urgency of the business need to justify risk-taking. This equation is unlikely to happen of its own accord and will need managing, and creating this kind of balance in a large organisation can be very difficult. Over a long period of time these desirable values, although essential for future success, tend to become ossified. Paternalistic com-panies find it very difficult to cease being paternalistic, even when that approach becomes self defeating.

The problems and opportunities for businesses differ from country to country. Each country has a different history, educational system, social conventions, national characteristics and levels of aspiration. These bear down heavily on the individual, and I have observed over the years that most of us carry clear 'tracking' signs of our background and upbringing. These may be ameliorated or changed by long periods of living and working in other countries or other groups of people but the 'Englishness', 'Welshness', 'Frenchness' or 'Germanness' of the individual seldom disappears altogether. All these factors mean that it is impossible to outline single approaches or actions which will lead to the sort of changes and success we are seeking. It is extremely dangerous to generalise. There is as big a difference between the best and the worst of British businesses as there is between British, Japanese and American companies. However, in this area of generating the real power that people can bring to an organisation or enterprise every group will respond to different approaches. The best one can hope to do under these circumstances is to try to describe the processes at work and debate some of the issues which need attention.

It is my belief that in the United Kingdom we have greater opportunities for change and improvement, both for individuals and for our country, than in most other countries. I make no apology for believing that most of our people are of very high calibre. Despite the pleasure we seem to derive from continually harping on our inadequacies, or the characteristics which we dislike, we still retain a number of key characteristics which are widely appreciated and envied. We are basically a tolerant society which respects the individual and we have high creative capabilities – as evidenced by our relative success in invention and the achievement of Nobel prizes. Most of us have latent scientific and technical capabilities which, although undeveloped, are still there, plain for all to see. Although there are specific pockets of other countries (e.g. California) where young people have even greater computer awareness than in the United Kingdom, as a rule our young people are comfortable with computers and, thanks to one of our rare educational successes, they are open to the use of information technology. We have many of the essential building-blocks for success and yet we utilise the abilities of our people uniquely badly. For a variety of reasons our educational system has tended to be elitist and, to borrow a phrase which I admire, we educate for failure. Our failure to raise self-esteem and self-belief in our youth is enhanced by the (thankfully dying) legacies of our class system. Even though I have lived through a revolution in social mobility, the United Kingdom is still characterised by people who believe that, by reason of birth, education, opportunity or background, many of life's prizes are beyond their reach. Anyone who has worked with American, German and British workforces knows that every American, and most Germans, believe that they are capable of doing any job within the organisation – including that of chairman. It is only in Britain that we apply self-selected limits to our capabilities and these, together with our lack of belief in training and our general attitudes to work and business, have held us back in the World Olympics of business success. However, the very fact that we have not tackled these problems opens tremendous opportunities if we can get to grips with the underlying difficulties.

If we are to change our approach, there seem to me to be three key actions we have to take. The first is that we have to open up the whole debate and argument on how to enable our people to perform closer to their real abilities. This should be a subject for discussion, analysis and experimentation and will involve changes in attitude and approach in most areas of our social fabric and activity. From my travels around the United Kingdom, I get the feeling that people are increasingly aware that these changes simply have to be made if we are to achieve greater economic and social success.

The second field of action is, I believe, that we must shift the whole basis of leadership, motivation and administration towards the encouragement of the individual and away from the bureaucratic treatment of groups. Treating people as groups is almost entirely for the benefit of the administration. We can hope to succeed as businesses and as a country only when each individual is operating as close to the limits of his or her ability as is possible. As I travel around the country in my retirement, I am horrified and depressed at the sheer waste of human capability which I encounter in almost every area of activity. It is not just the scandal of our levels of unemployment, or the problems we have in adjusting from declining industries to new. Everywhere I go I see people working hard, but with a level of effectiveness greatly below what they are capable of and, as a result, suffering from frustration, boredom and lack of involvement.

The last area where we simply have to change as companies is in our responsibility for people. It is up to us to create some order and consistency of the framework within which people work. At present, because we so seldom look at these things in an holistic way, we have created disparities and inconsistencies between the administrative systems, the management, the company's values and its business aims. These disparities make it difficult for our people to give their best.

The task of managing and leading people is much more akin to being the conductor of an orchestra or a large band or the producer of a film, than being an engineer assembling and running a machine or an accountant. A carefully selected, trained and conducted orchestra brings new meaning and interpretation to a well-loved piece of music. Moreover, each player gains from the others and they find themselves playing beyond their personal achievements in individual practice. A concert is much more than the sum of its parts; the interaction with the audience, the effect of the concert hall and the whole ambience are all parts of the conductor's repertoire which enable him or her to achieve a unique and soaring performance. The performance takes on a life of its own, each part of the experience influences the others to create a spiral of encouragement and an experience simultaneously uplifting, transforming and exhausting for everyone concerned – the players, the audience and, of course, the conductor himself. So it is with managing a group of

19

people. Conditions can be created where the whole outfit buzzes, where everyone works to keep and improve the momentum of the whole and people look forward to further success. These exciting results depend, in business or in orchestral music, on the conductor and how he has gone about his job; how he has selected his people, what standards he expects from them, what practice and training he undertakes and how he encourages or corrects individuals. None of this happens automatically or by accident – and the successful manager of a successful enterprise will have to pay every bit as much attention to the creation and training of his own 'orchestra'. He will be conscious of the need to relate to his 'audience' – the customer; and he will be careful to tune in to the 'concert hall' – the environment in which the business is being conducted. He makes sure he gets plenty of advice on the technicalities of playing the various 'instruments', be it production, design, research or accountancy. The final results depend upon the people whom he selects, trains, rehearses and coaches – but ultimately each has to play his or her own part. Just as a concert can be wrecked by one player so can a business. The aim has to be to get everyone working together, each individual playing superbly but in perfect harmony with the others. It is the manager who pulls them all together so that they make more than the sum of the individual parts.

I have been encouraged to write this book to draw on my experience to outline some of the practical things which might be done to start us down this path. My views are not meant to be prescriptive. As in everything else I have done, written or talked about, my hope is that a comment, example or thought will strike a responsive chord. I hope that others may be made aware of these problems and be encouraged to begin producing their own solutions. The room for improvement is so vast and the rewards so great that even a tiny tilt of attention to this critical and key area of human activity will have enormous results. The great thing about improving the ways we relate to each other in organisations, and the way we discharge our responsibility for 'managing' people, is that it is a 'win-win' situation. Our companies can win only if the individuals within them are winning. There are no losers in this field of trying to improve our skills both individually and collectively.

TWO The Values

No one is ever in doubt when a business is in overdrive: suddenly you have the initiative and the whole business begins to hum. Problems cease to be problems and are viewed as opportunities. Less time and effort is necessary to achieve commitment to the actions being taken and the business begins to take off. The extraordinary thing about this process is that ultimately the business truly begins to run itself. As your people's confidence in their ability to deliver increases they will continually seek more demanding goals. Nothing will be beyond their reach. Ultimately the chief executive of a business in overdrive feels that his staff are the ones pushing him, rather than him being the continuous spur to everybody else. This process, which is so rewarding for everybody concerned, is the absolute key to releasing energy and increasing capability. Although I write primarily of business, the same phenomenon can be observed in the armed services, schools, the public sector (particularly in local government, where I can think of a number of examples of local authorities who astonish themselves by what they are able to achieve), charities and in almost any activity which involves the freely given commitment of individual and active-minded men and women.

The starting point to achieve this managerial nirvana lies in ensuring that the value systems of the business are congruent with the values and aspirations of the individuals. These values are the glue that holds the whole thing together. The values which permeate an organisation from top to bottom produce the invisible framework which substitutes for continuous control and perennial hands-on meddling with tiny details. The values system should engender trust and confidence and should force more and more clarity. As Tom Peters demonstrated, the value system transcends business situations and eventually permeates the beliefs of practically everybody in the organisation. It acts as an invisible quality standard as well as a constant reference point and spur and, because values can seldom be absolute, it represents a crawling ratchet of self-improvement. Even though the values are durable, their application in different circumstances requires constant adaptation, application and thought. The value system is the basis for the whole relationship of a business with its people, and of its people with one another. The value system is one of the prime means of transferring the ownership of problems to your people. The integrity of the system will then be enforced by the people themselves, rather than by a police force of supervisors or quality checkers. Values are also an invisible recruiting sergeant: people are often attracted to join a firm because of their perception of the sort of outfit it is, and are therefore likely to attract people who share your basic values.

Despite the fact that values are such an integral part of any business, it is extraordinary how few approach the question in any logical or systematic way. In practically all instances organisations derive their values from particular individuals and their aspirations, and in many cases the values will persist from generation to generation. In the services these are called traditions, and the whole regimental system is based upon perennial reinforcement of the values established in the past. Not for nothing did Admiral Cunningham persist in sending ships to evacuate the army from Crete, despite horrendous losses, using the argument that the traditions of the Royal Navy as a reliable support for its fellow services warranted the loss of life and risks being taken by his fleet.

The values of businesses are usually embedded in their history and derive frequently from those who set up the company in the first place. Thereafter they tend to develop a self re-enforcing quality. Employees who appear to empathise with the values of the group are selected and indeed individuals seek companies whose values they admire. Iconoclasts are unwelcome and are made to know it in the very early days. Peer groups tend to ostracise those who do not fit in and in business, where success depends on working with others, people who do not join in find it difficult to get things done. But values need to change and evolve. IBM's values derived directly from Thomas Watsons views and concepts, which were so detailed and so rigorously applied that even expected styles of dress were maintained for years after the business changed. There could hardly be greater

25

apparent differences between the values of IBM and, say, Apple Computers, and differences are immediately apparent in approach and values between, say, Royal Dutch Shell, with its emphasis on internationally mobile teams of expatriates, and Texaco, with its emphasis on American control.

The concerns of a company the size of ICI for its people, its wish to be leaders of management ideas and the relationship and involvement of its people in them, derives from the personal values of its founding fathers, Brunner and Mond. They had been long dead by the time I joined the company and yet their ideas continued to influence the company every bit as strongly as in their own day. Time and again I blessed the belief in people and their development which imbued my company.

Grand Metropolitan is one of the few companies I know which has actually tried continually to codify and express its values system, and derives these largely from the characteristics of its chairman, Lord Allen Sheppard. A company which claims to thrive on high achievement and high stress, never to be satisfied with its achievements, to be restless and to care for its people and for the communities in which it operates, directly reflects Allen's own approach and views. What has particularly interested me about that company is that it has changed its thrust and direction markedly over the last years and has grown at a spanking pace by acquisition, meanwhile rationalising its business profile through disposals and dispersals. Other businesses they have acquired have adopted the style of Grand Metropolitan within a short time, and this applies whether the acquired company is in

Africa or America. Because their approach to a problem starts from a shared belief, which is the basis of the company's success so far, they do not have to proselytise the approach. Everybody in the company lives it every day. Nobody believes that anything is unachievable and everyone knows success is what matters and that no one is interested in sophisticated reasons for failure.

Similarly the very special features of speed and informality that characterise Virgin derive directly from Richard Branson's characteristics and beliefs, and mean that the company is willing to tackle anyone and anything, regardless of size. I have chosen one example from the distant past and two where values systems are being set up at the present time. I have no doubt that long after Richard or Allen have dropped their responsibilities their companies will continue to have similar characteristics. With any luck these will endure as long as the influence of Brunner and Mond has upon ICI, and be as fruitful and rewarding, both for the people in the company and for those who have had the foresight to invest in them.

Although in most cases business values derive from the beliefs and philosophy of a leader or leaders at a specific period of time, it is essential that the values of the company reflect both the business needs and competitive characteristics of that business. This happens in the first place by a process of self-selection because, unless the philosophy of the leader is appropriate to his business, the company will not grow and prosper because the values will not have time to entrench themselves as the foundation for future success.

However, if you are setting up a business on a green-field basis, or if it has lost its way or needs re-positioning in some way, it is important to think carefully about the characteristics that will give you a reasonable chance of sustainable competitive advantage. Remember that values are long lasting – they take time to permeate an organisation and, once established, they can be flexed but are difficult to change or eradicate altogether. If part of the values system has involved continual experimentation and pushing restlessly at the frontiers of knowledge and risk, this may be an ideal basis for success in a fast developing field such as electronics. Indeed, these are essential characteristics for those businesses. If, however, one is running a hospital, I doubt whether one would choose that particular combination of experimentation and risk. I would be happier to go to a hospital whose value system involved words like concerned, sensitive and reliable, rather than one which, in its restless urge to stay ahead, was prepared to accept the risk-taking involved. Obviously, different types of businesses need specific value systems to retain competitive success – it does not take a genius to see that chemical companies not concerned about the environment are unlikely to survive for long. If you want a business to reflect these concerns, you had better make sure that you recruit people who value nature and have a proper respect for the universe which is our host. By definition these broad concepts are reflected clearly in the interests, concerns and ways in which people go about their daily lives. It is far better to build concern about them into one's values than to attempt to enforce environmental compliance by imposing rules on people whose hearts are not in the objectives.

A value statement is in essence a personality profile of the company, and hence of the people in it. It is an open declaration of the attitudes and personal characteristics admired and considered essential for business success. But it is much more than that. As I have said the expressed values in a company attract people comfortable with that sort of existence; those who seek to join a particular company with a well-expressed value system are likely to be those who believe in that approach to life. Those who do not wish to live a high-stress, high-achievement, willing-to-tackle-anything sort of life are unlikely to apply to join Grand Metropolitan. Those wary of tackling large issues and who prefer a formal structure are unlikely to want to work for Virgin. Thus, a clear sense of corporate values can be not only an attraction but a self-policing repellent. People who do not like the style of the company will vote with their feet, without having to be pushed, because few people of worth are willing to sublimate their lives to working in organisations they do not believe in or feel comfortable in. Indeed, why should they? We spend more of our time at work than we do with our families. We go to infinite trouble to choose our marriage partner, often taking into consideration the same issues, such as congruence of interests and values, which we should be considering when choosing a company. Ultimately, long after the existing leaders have left, the value system of a company will provide a checklist for the personality profile of future leaders, and continue to attract people who possess the characteristics which the company believes essential for its success.

However, there is a trap in all of this. The moment may come when the old values need to be changed, and this can be very difficult. It takes a long time to bed them in and an equally long time to ensure that they are changed beyond the possibility of bouncing back. I used to believe that it was possible to produce a momentum of change which would be self-perpetuating, but on a number of recent occasions I have witnessed the amount of time it takes to embed new beliefs in a large organisation. My predecessor as chairman of an ICI Division, Jack Lofthouse, and I tried to change the value system of that outfit, initially known as the Heavy Organic Chemical Division. We both wanted a more open, faster moving, more risk-taking outfit, with higher aspirations – all of which involved changes of attitude and systems. When we started, we employed or were responsible for about 9000 people, so the task did not seem impossible. Despite unremitting effort to break the bureaucratic and conformist approach of the division, we only began to make progress after nearly three years of effort. I left at the end of five years when I was unexpectedly appointed to the main board, and I was succeeded by a fine manager, but a traditionalist. Within two years the old habits had returned and at least half our efforts to change things had been dissipated. There is a curious continuity of corporate memory which is resistant to change. I believe that five years of sustained, concentrated and skilful effort is the minimum necessary to change a long-established value system. The difficulty is that although company values will, and probably should, have a long life, it is all too easy for them to become fixed – like flies in amber. When that happens a company can rapidly lose the ability to keep up with the rest of the world. Both IBM and General Motors had extremely strong corporate cultures, which had stood them in good stead in the past. Neither culture, however, was able to adapt sufficiently fast to the hurricane of change which is upon us now.

It is therefore necessary to take a fresh look at the culture and values of your company from time to time and rigorously to question their relevance, not only to the world of today but to the world we are probably moving into tomorrow. When you wish to introduce a change of value it needs to be a clear decision, enunciated and demonstrated by example over and over again. When I took over as chairman of ICI, my colleagues and I were concerned about the level of conformity which our well-established culture had produced throughout the company, across the world. We believed it was unlikely that such a strong culture should be equally applicable through the manifold areas of business where we were then operating. These were far broader, both in range of product and in geographical dispersion, than our forefathers had envisaged or sought to cope with. One of our early decisions, therefore, was to try to encourage difference within the company – difference of approach, of attitude and of style. One would have thought that it needed only a nod in these directions for people's individuality to take over, and that the constituent businesses would gallop in different

31

directions with the speed of light. In the event, it proved necessary almost to *force* different approaches in different parts of the business. This process has now been followed to its logical conclusion by the split of the parent company into two, each of which will retain something of the company's original culture but will develop its own forward sense of values, more appropriate to the businesses they are operating.

Writing a statement of values is likely to lead one into the same trap which the mission statements produced by practically all companies over the past years have fallen into. I am strong believer in a mission statement, as indeed I am a believer in a statement of values, but the difficulty is that both can become a soft consensus of terms acceptable to everybody. Most of us could write an all purpose mission or value statement in any bar on a Tuesday night, which could apply to any company in the world. Indeed many show signs of having been written by committees and honed until any area of contention has been removed. But statements of values are, after all, codes of belief and behaviour and involve making hard choices clearly and unambiguously. They are bound to be contentious if they are to be worth anything. It does not take a great deal of thought to understand that it is necessary to distinguish between trying to run a marathon or a relay sprint, and that the approaches to training, preparation and physical and mental characteristics are different. It does not require long hours of meetings at every level in the company to recognise that change and flexibility are not the same as consistency, reliability and predictability, that high achievement and risk taking are incompatible with the avoidance of failure, and so on. When making a statement of values you need to check continuously that you are prepared to reject the opposite of what you are selecting for the basis of your future business. You should not waste time enunciating the obvious.

Honesty, quality and attention to the customer are givens for every sort of business and organisation, but this does not mean there are no circumstances where you would not include any of those three characteristics in your statement. If you are in a business which has enjoyed a monopoly for a great many years and may be careless of its attention to the customer's interest, your value statement needs to underline, in every manner you can find, the necessity for customer care and sensitivity to the customer's needs. If you are in a business where the competitive ethics are questionable, and you believe that you can survive by operating in a different way, stress that your business will be run to the highest ethical and moral standards. However, do not make such a claim unless you are prepared to live up to it. It may seem fine to the outside world, but your people will know if it is a sham and they will then lose their belief in the business. Of course the problem is that everyone always wants every-thing and that devising a value statement is like writing a job description – you can easily end up with a fine pen portrait of Superman. Values, if they are to motivate, are about choices, because there are only a limited number of values you can hope to demonstrate consistently day in, day out.

The essence of a value statement is that your people will continuously test themselves, you, your colleagues, the systems and the actions of the company against the values professed. It is not a bit of use saying that you wish to run an open company, unless the board and the chairman will welcome the barrage of criticism which should properly be unleashed – and not only welcome it, but pay attention and endeavour to meet the concerns expressed. The ultimate aim is to produce a single-sentence statement encompassing the key characteristics of the type of company you are and wish to become. It is the points of *difference* from other companies or the areas where particular attention is needed that must be stressed. At all costs avoid 'weasel words', which purport to say one thing but are really designd to obscure the harshness of the point. However it is perfectly permissible to use short-hand terms in a value statement. For example the word 'professionalism' signifies high standards, the necessity for continual improvement, learning and the pursuit of excellence in every aspect of your business. A value statement which is going to be any use will highlight areas of confrontation, will bring problems out in the open and attack them in order to turn them into opportunities. It will be about grabbing the initiative and going actively for solutions, rather than hoping that time will alleviate or remove the problems you have identified. The reality of life is that time probably will resolve most problems, if only by forcing you out of the business, but that is not the same as going hell for leather after anything you think is standing in your way.

34

The value statement must address not only problems but the attitudes to employees.

Of course, when faced with the consequences of statements of values, the temptation is to water them down or produce lengthier and lengthier descriptions of what it is that you mean. But the essence of a value statement is that there can be little compromise. If safety comes first, you have to be willing to shut down an unsafe plant on the spot, regardless of the commercial and financial consequences. If people come first, you may have to be prepared to accept considerable short-term commercial disadvantage in the long-term interests of your people, and so on.

I have long admired the American company 3M. They seem to me to be one of the small number of highly successful companies who have managed almost to institutionalise creativity and the development of new products and ideas. (How did any of us exist before Post-its?) If you talk to them about this continued success they attribute it, I believe rightly, to the principles they apply to managing their people. There are four, and they do not differ much from the principles many other companies claim to espouse. They are:

    i. to respect the dignity and work of individuals
    ii. to encourage the initiative of each employee
    iii. to challenge individual capabilities
    iv. to provide equal opportunity for development.

The difference from other companies is that the 3M management believe in them totally and follow them in detail, day in and day out. They are not new and they have endured

35

through many changes of management. But the way in which they have been applied, and the detailed follow-up systems supporting them, have continually evolved and altered. The stress on the individual and the recognition that risk-taking and innovation are requirements for growth are reflected in the way the company deals with its highly motivated and successful workforce. The well-known story of the development of the ubiquitous 'Post-it' note is a splendid example of the practical appliance of these beliefs. The initial invention was a failure – an adhesive which did not fix permanently but retained its 'stickiness'. The inventor, a 3M employee, used it privately to put reminders on personal documents and was encouraged by the company to develop the idea further. It is now a worldwide business, successful in its own right.

These principles sound like motherhood and apple pie. But many value statements surprise those who are not involved in the business. For example the SAS Regiment of the British Army have a four-point value system which derives from their founder, David Stirling, in the last war. Two of the values one would expect, but how many of us would expect the third to be 'democracy' and the fourth to be 'humility and humour'? Yet I, and many others, can attest to the applications of these unlikely military virtues at every level of that excellent organisation. When you reflect that they were chosen as two of four guidelines for an organisation founded in 1942 it is even more astonishing. Most Service organisations at that time were anything but democratic – and humility was an attribute many of us achieved thorough inadequacy but few sought as a key to professional and self-improvement. All too many outfits think that merely writing down fine words will get the job done. The reality is the reverse. Unless the values are lived up to at every level, unless the systems support the values, unless those who are promoted are seen to espouse and buy into the concepts, value statements are a massive switch off.

I am wary of written value statements for that reason, but that is not an excuse for not spending time thinking through the sort of values you want and the directions in which you want the values to change. In an ideal world values are the common currency of a business and you put into words the practice you have followed and which is instantly recognised by your employees and the outside world. Most value statements emanate from the chief executive – and indeed should – but it is of the greatest possible importance that, if the chief executive produces a statement you do not believe he can live up to, he should be challenged quickly. The first approach to a value statement by a chief executive should therefore often start as a private check-list of the style he wants, both for himself and for his outfit, and he must be a continuous example of that style. This is not easy and is an additional reason why I believe that value statements should be short and encompass no more than four or five points. The difficulty of living by them is that the chief executive is on duty twenty-four hours a day and 365 days a year. A display of intolerance in a pub or a failure to listen carefully to a contrary view because one is tired or distracted can

37

have the same damaging effects as an ill-judged notice or letter to the employees. Because there is usually little mutuality of trust in a business, values are viewed with cynicism and the expectation is that they are for external consumption rather than as a credo for life.

By the time they become a CEO most people will have found the style they are comfortable with and can live with. However, real problems occur when one's business requires approaches one is not familiar or naturally at ease with. For example, if your analysis shows that the business needs to be more flexible, while you know that you are only comfortable in a structured, no-surprise type of environment you need to think very carefully about whether you are in the right job. Of course it is possible to change aspects of one's personal style, but usually only by Herculean strength of will, and doing so takes time and may require help. If you decide that you must become more flexibly minded, it is probably better to approach this as one of your personal objectives and ask your colleagues to point out to you when you are behaving in a rigid fashion. When they do and they will (sometimes with relish!) – you have to be genuinely grateful and try to adjust. People at the top are often worried by this sort of thing and sometimes feel that it is a sign of weakness and lack of fitness for the job. They worry that such public awareness will harm their authority and their ability to lead. However, this is to misread the whole situation. You are trying to change yourself because you believe your company needs to behave in a different way. Change starts at the top and by example, and the public demonstration of your personal commitment to change is a valuable encouragement to others.

Like so many other aspects of leadership, this approach calls for self-discipline, moral courage and clarity of purpose. If you cannot undertake the changes you consider necessary for the group as a whole, you should make the break and move on. If you do not, not only will *you* fail but so will the company. Fortunately, life seldom presents too many of these challenges at one time, since it is impossible to up-skittle the value system of a company at one go.

The enduring nature of the primary values is imbued in you all – as in 3M or the SAS. You joined your company because of them and they have been reinforced by your experience and the behaviour of your colleagues. It may be necessary to change the application of those values and occasionally you may have to try consciously to steer towards a new one – such as our striving in ICI for organisational and behavioural difference. Only when you have been living the values yourself and have observed them throughout the company is it safe to write them down. Only then can such a written code be helpful, instead of posing a major risk of losing credibility, trust and belief. The reality is that every group of people must have a shared set of values – if this is not so they do not exist as a group. The skill required is not only to recognise this fact, but to build on and enhance the values which will be helpful to future success and to work hard to eliminate the unsuccessful ones. This calls for you to think your way through the whole of your business needs and to make a real and continuous

39

effort to manage the changes which are going to be required. The difference from other business situations is that these 'soft' issues involve emotions and deeply held beliefs. Working on corporate values calls for sensitivity and persistence, but such work is essential if your company is to adjust to the changing world and to prosper.

THREE The Musicians

If the single most important factor for the success of a business is the capability and performance of the people within it, it follows that the process of selection must be one of the most important exercises in the business calendar. From the point of view of the individual, selection of the company or business you aim to join is without question one of the key milestones in your life. Even though it is now unlikely that any individual will work for only one business throughout his or her life, there are limits to the number of employers one can have without appearing to be a rolling stone incapable of staying anywhere for any length of time.

The whole process of applying for jobs and selecting people warrants a great deal of careful thinking. It is surprising that in many companies the thought given to the process and the attention and time devoted to it is so rudimentary. Substantial amounts of time are often spent only on the selection of managers or future managers, but when it comes to recruiting for junior posts or shop-floor positions most British companies follow rather superficial recruitment procedures. This is in marked contrast to the attention given

41

by the Japanese to this important aspect of business management. Just as Japanese companies apply a far greater proportion of time and money to the training and development of their people, so they approach the recruitment of individuals at every level with the degree of thoroughness and attention to detail which characterises their management approach in general.

The selection of people is one of those tasks which, in an ideal world, should not be delegated at all, but, if delegation is essential because of the size of the outfit, results of that delegation need to be assessed continually, on both an objective and a subjective basis. Moreover, those to whom the responsibility is delegated should be carefully chosen and prepared for the task; they may well require special training. No matter how systematised selection procedures are, it seems to me that the ability to assess the ultimate potential of individuals after a relatively short exposure to them is a gift. Most companies and organisations have an individual who has established a formidable track record for being able to spot latent talent. Where there is such a skill, it is worthwhile making full use of his or her abilities. Selection of people is almost always better done as a group rather than by an individual, but the 'talent spotter' can be employed as a roving member of all selection teams. Over the years ICI were lucky enough to find a number of people who possess this particular form of sixth sense and a totally disproportionate number of the ultimate leadership of that company had been recruited by the same people. The question of selection is quite different from that of subsequent development. The particular skills and abilities involved in spotting potential winners are not necessarily the same as those which encourage the young neophyte to develop into the mature all-rounder whom everybody is seeking.

As in so many other areas of business, selection is easier in small companies than in large. The owner of a small business will see, judge and select almost every person who is to join the company for every available position. Organisations benefit enormously from this consistency of approach and judgement. The larger the company becomes the more desirable it is to try to emulate the techniques of selection which are a natural feature of the small company. It must always be remembered that, although selection is usually for a specific post or task, in reality you are choosing future members of the team and, indeed, hoping to choose future leaders of the team. Most organisations seek to develop their future leadership from within their ranks and there are good reasons, quite apart from laziness and expense, why this should be so. Recruiting from outside is always a risk, where you are staking your judgement on a series of interviews and tests, together with a written history provided by the individual himself. References are unlikely to give the bad news, although a skilful reference reader may detect any omissions – usually the only clear pointer to the weaknesses you are looking for. There is, therefore, a great deal less risk in choosing an individual whom you have seen operating for a long period of time, and whose characteristics, good and bad, you can evaluate more clearly.

Apart from the risk element there are other reasons why

businesses try to develop their own future leadership. Firstly few people relish having to train and develop a boss recruited from outside, who spends his first months having to learn the ropes of the organisation which he has just joined. Secondly, one of the key motivators for individuals is recognition and in Britain there is a belief that recognition is particularly associated with promotion. The knowledge that there is no possibility of further advancement is enough to make many people consider voting with their feet. A good company should be continually investing in its people, but if you do this your people need to feel that there is scope and opportunity for them to utilise the skills and capabilities they are so painfully developing. Thirdly there is a measurable cost involved in duff selections. It takes time before it is obvious that a wrong choice has been made. For the first year or so in a company the individual will inevitably be performing below full potential and the company will be investing heavily in training and developing individual skills and teaching him or her appropriate ways of functioning. If, at a later stage, the individual proves inadequate for the task, this represents a substantial misspent cost to the business. Of course it also represents wasted effort and a lost opportunity to recruit and develop somebody else, as well as a distressing experience of failure for the individual concerned.

It is not possible to quantify exactly the costs involved in a mistake, but they are considerably more than the direct measurable costs. For a start, there is the money involved in the selection procedure, the diversion of management time in training and the extra management time before you accept that there is no silk purse to be made from this particular sow's ear. There are the overhead costs associated with every individual, together with some sort of severance payment. But all these measurable costs – say between twice and three times the salary paid – are dwarfed by the loss of the profit expected to be generated by the individual, and the even more serious loss of profit and momentum from those associated with him or her. There is an understandable vested interest in proving that the selection was not faulty; most failed selections survive for eighteen months or so and, when the notice period is added, one is often looking at a period of up to two years. It does not take a financial wizard to see that a mistake when choosing someone on, say, £25,000 per annum starting salary can amount to an unwanted extra cost of ten times that amount.

It is obviously important to try to get selection right first time and this can be achieved only by expending considerable care and effort, and approaching the whole business with a high degree of professionalism. Since I came from a Services background, I have always tended to contrast the time and effort they put into the selection of future officers with how the average business goes about the selection of its management. The Services still recruit practically all their intake of young men and women at, or even before, graduate age. However most Services use 'professional' selection boards, which involve two or three days of events; interviews, tests, practical exposure to working in teams, observation on the ability to work with others, demands for written and verbal reports on situations, and so on. Even after initial selection most other specialist functions within the Services demand equally rigorous selection systems. Watching the selection process of the Royal Marines, for example, or more particularly the SAS, who are recruiting officers with a proven track record from within the ranks of the army, makes one realise how important selection should be. The SAS procedure takes place over a two-month period of exposure to every possible type of hurdle. Little wonder that only about two out of every hundred applicants make it in the end.

The approach of most businesses is almost the opposite of this exhaustive, and exhausting, process. Typically, there is an advertisement describing a specific job, almost entirely in terms of the task to be done. In addition to limiting the numbers of people who will reply by concentrating on this one job alone, most business advertisements also narrow down further the potential candidates by giving a list of 'essential' requirements. These will include 'essential' experience, some indications on age and, frequently, precise requirements for academic and/or professional qualifications. Most are designed to restrict the number of people requiring to be seen and most of them are, I suggest, more for the administrative convenience of the selectors than an open-minded attempt to ensure that the best possible individual is recruited. The omissions from this list are almost as striking as the 'closing down' nature of the advertisement. They seldom include a list of the characteristics sought. It would be perfectly possible, for example, to mention that the job requires initiative and that candidates will need to indicate areas where they have shown initiative, drive and imagination. Many jobs require persistence; again it is not beyond the wit of man to ask a candidate to give examples of persistence to achieve what they have wanted to do. There is seldom any description of the human qualities required and, although the responsibilities of the job and specific tasks are usually well described, the opportunities for change and improvement and the potential challenge afforded by working in the company are hardly ever outlined. Given the diffidence and lack of self-belief of many British people, it is not surprising that most people who read job adverts decide that they would not be suitable for the job. Nor is it unusual if the initial selection from the painstakingly written application forms is done by a secretary, on the basis of ticking those which fall inside the prescribed limits. Is this really the way for a company to ensure that it is seeing the best potential people with the highest long-term capability?

When considering this whole area of selection, it is necessary to start with the company's policy on staffing. Most companies aim to recruit young people straight from school or university, who are malleable and have not picked up 'bad habits' elsewhere. Steady recruitment of school leavers or university graduates is in any event essential if one is to have a reasonable age spread within the company. After all, the primary objective of a business is survival, and everybody hopes that they are setting up businesses which will last for generations. This can be achieved only if people are available

47

in the appropriate age brackets to pass the relay baton on for the future. If the intention is to recruit at school-leaving age, say, half the number of people you will need to cover your needs for future expansion and inevitable natural wastage, the most important thing to consider is what is a sustainable and steady rate of intake. If you are interested in attracting the best young people (and all this effort is worthwhile if that is your aim) you will need to develop links and contacts with schools, universities, sixth form colleges etc, who are dealing with a continual stream of young people. They will naturally give preference to those employers they know will take, say, one or two graduates every academic year, rather than those who want nobody at all for five years and then call upon them suddenly for five or six. I am less sure than I used to be whether competition for the brightest and best is so intense that companies will again find it necessary to put their stamp on young people at an early stage of their development – before they go to university for instance. Very few companies seem to be sponsoring graduates today and, indeed, even when such sponsorship took place, it was always a high-risk operation from the point of view of the company. You cannot actually tie someone to you; all you can do is hope that you have selected your people so carefully that they will feel an obligation to work with you for some time after completing their sponsored course. If they do not feel that obligation you are probably well shot of them, since they are not likely to be the stuff you need. It seems to me more likely that in the future companies will try to attract the best young people by giving career talks, by the adoption of schools by factories and by other links on a less direct and selective basis than the sponsorship which had its heyday in the fifties and sixties.

As well as consistency of ideas about how many young people one is seeking to recruit, and how often, provision must be made within the company for promoting people from the shop floor. ICI had an enviable record for this. Indeed some of its very best people, including contemporaries of mine, had joined the company as apprentices, had been sponsored through to degrees, taken on as managers and so on, the whole way through the company. In the future the distinction between the technologically skilled and the academically qualified will weaken, and desirably so. Nothing in my experience says that every manager has to have a university degree – although most of us would be glad if we had. The lack of specific plans and positive effort to enable good people – either late starters or those who have not had earlier educational opportunities – to rise through the company is another area where business contrasts unfavourably with the Services. The fact is that every business needs the best talent, wherever it may be found, and people who have been given such opportunities – as well as knowing their business backwards – have a commitment to and concern for the company which is priceless. However, it is an equal pitfall to decide that everybody must be developed from within your own 'stock' of shop floor and graduate recruits. There are real dangers in areas of high specialisation, such as information technology or accountancy, if nobody is ever brought in from outside. You

49

can reasonably hope to be kept abreast of the latest theoretical thinking by the recruitment of top flight graduates from the best business schools and universities, but this infusion of new ideas at the bottom is not necessarily strong enough to prevent ossification setting in, unless people at the top of the specialised field are open minded. Specialist organisations which are entirely self-staffed run real risks of becoming incestuous and believing that only they have the philosopher's stone. I like to see a small but regular intake of people from other organisations towards the top of these areas. When recruiting in this way, it is important to be absolutely clear that you are looking for not only a first-class person, but one who comes from an organisation whose prowess in that area you respect. This may well mean that you will have to head-hunt a specific individual rather than rely upon open advertisement. If you want to poach a competitor's staff it is sensible to make the approach through an intermediary – and preferably a professional one.

Overall the aim of any good company must be to be a net exporter of people; indeed, if the excellence of your selection and subsequent development of your people is right this will be inevitable, because you will always be producing more 'people power' inside your organisation than even the most ambitious, sustainable expansion can cope with. Although this is certainly true for a large company, for a small, rapidly growing company the limitations on growth are likely to be the rate at which you can develop and recruit people within the mould of the company's values. Many organisations worry that being a net exporter is a demonstration

50

of profligacy and waste but I have never believed this to be the case. For a great many years the Ford Motor Company appeared to provide a totally disproportionate share of skilled accountants in British business, and similar roles in other areas and management skills have been filled by Shell and ICI at different periods in their development. The key to being a net exporter, of course, should be that the people exported are the ones who you do not mind losing. If you are continually losing the very people you wanted to keep to ensure the growth of your own company, then a bit of 'navel gazing' is in order, because you are obviously failing to provide the opportunities and the stretch necessary to hold the best. But if you consistently produce more skilled people than you require for your needs there are significant advantages in terms of the company's reputation in their moving elsewhere. For example it soon becomes known that *the* place to have studied production management is Mars. Mars have, by the excellence of their managerial approach produced a stream of extremely able production management, imbued with fervour for continual improvement, long before the Japanese made these words fashionable. To have such a reputation ensures that people who are thinking of following a particular career will attempt to join your company and you are therefore in an advantageous position to recruit from those with the best potential. Of course, this does not necessarily mean that you will get it right, but if they do not even offer themselves for selection it is difficult indeed to produce the winning team. Moreover the fact that people are constantly leaving you to better themselves, and

51

evidently do, is a potent source of pressure for success on your own managers and on you. You know you will hold your selected tigers only if you provide plenty of game for them to hunt, and that, in turn, increases the pace and excellence of your organisation.

It is of the greatest importance when selecting people to be clear that you are not just trying to fill a single job. A moment's reflection will show you that it is useless to try to appoint a man or woman at the age of, say, thirty-five to fill a job, with the conviction that there is no other job they will be able to do. You will inevitably be forced to move them at some time in the future, or be lumbered with somebody who has lost their basic drive, and is increasingly 'time serving' in the job slot you sought to fill. You should look for somebody who is not only well able to do the job you have in mind but has the potential for onward movement, either within that field or in more general areas of managerial activity. Increasingly what will be needed in the future are people with specialised skills, but who have a 'helicopter pilot' overview of all the activities of the business. The narrow specialist, who is an absolute expert in his own field, is becoming unusable because almost everything now has to be done by teams and you are looking for specialist input into that team, combined with some understanding of the other fields of activity. By definition, such input means give-and-take and an understanding of the constraints and opportunities of other fields of specialisation. One should be looking for both characteristics – ability to achieve excellence in a field of specialisation, and ability to take a wide view, encompassing not only the financial aspects of the business but technology, markets, customers and the external environment. Filling a particular slot with an individual who has only one of these characteristics not only creates a blockage but represents a wasted opportunity.

My own experiences of recruitment have been mixed and I do not think I am a natural talent spotter during interviews. I have had failures at the expense, I fear, of those I selected when trying to choose people with unusual backgrounds and skills in an effort to change the values and operating characteristics of departments or businesses for which I have been responsible. For these purposes I usually found it more effective to choose people whom I had been able to observe, albeit obliquely, at work for a period of time, who were already skilled and comfortable with the changes I wanted to make. Imaginative appointing and use of individuals within one's own outfit is an easier and quite different skill from recruitment from different organisations, industries or universities.

Recruiting a new individual is a chance to shift the balance of the company as a whole, so it is important that you bear in mind where you are trying to take the company. Business is a microcosm of the world in which it operates and it is desirable, therefore, to have people who are interested in all facets of the world scene. Of course perfect balance is never achievable, but every company needs a balance between the 'doers' and the 'thinkers' – most people naturally incline towards one or the other characteristic. No company can afford to have solely 'doers', who are so keen for action that they never stop to think, or 'thinkers', so fascinated with theory that they never take positive action. There are many other pairs of balances which the ideal organisation should have – tacticians and strategists, for example; risk-takers and those blessed individuals who can foresee potential disasters to which others are blind. Outside recruitment is aimed at creating the team and characteristics you believe essential to business success. To make matters even more complex you are trying to think what you will need in five or six years' time and thereafter. You are looking for the balancing characteristics you need within the company as a whole. If you are trying to internationalise the business, it is as well to include a bias towards people who have shown interest in travel and working abroad, as well as those who have aptitude for languages. Buying in specific language skills is no longer so important for, with modern facilities, many languages can be learnt quite quickly.

Many of the personal characteristics you are seeking will derive from the values of the organisation. Even here, however, you may find that you need to tip the balance one way or another, and an infusion of new people always changes the overall nature of the team. This constant search for balance should not of course go as far as deliberately trying to inject contrary values, at variance with the old established ones. The selection procedure will in most cases save you from these extremes, but the danger is that you may lose the opportunity of adding a little salt or vinegar to the dish which enhances the flavour of the whole. In all of this you think not only of the good of your company but of the

54

interests of those you interview. Success for the individual is as much in the avoidance of joining an unsuitable company or group as in being offered the job and feeling that you have beaten the competition.

FOUR The Audition

When all the preparations have been made, the moment comes when you have to interview and select people. This is an area of considerable expertise and there is no doubt that one learns by experience, but it is important to be clear about what one is trying to do at the interviewing stage. The object of the exercise is to learn as much about the character, values and potential of the person as possible in a very limited period and in artificial circumstances. In a way the whole thing is a bit like a detective story, where you are looking for elusive clues to follow up, which will reveal more of the plot. It is important to remember that every candidate will inevitably be trying their hardest to make the best impression, and that few of them have any real idea of what it is that you are looking for – or what are plus or minus points in your eyes. Most candidates think that the interviewer is looking purely for the technical ability to do the job, combined with agreement with any views put forward by a superior. Very few realise that a robust defence of an idea in an interview is worth much more than submissive and often insincere agreement.

As in any good detective story, the various clues lead you to form a working hypothesis; the art then is to check whether your concept is correct. One needs to approach the same idea from a number of different directions to see whether the responses are consistent, or at minimum explicable. Very few people are consistent in everything they do; what you are really looking for is an indication whether there is a reasonable balance between the heart and the head. You certainly do not want, no matter how clever, a Mr Spock type thinking machine. There are few positions in business where such an individual can be utilised because business is about working with people, selling to people, buying from people – in fact relating to people the whole time. Relationships are based on emotion and not on logic – as all of us have experienced. However, emotion on its own can be as dangerous a characteristic as logic when the individual will have the fate and future well being of numbers of people in his or her hands. One wants people who can give of both their heart and their mind, having thought through the consequences, and are committed to whatever they do. This is where knowing their outside interests can be useful. The man who is interested in, for example, canoeing, and follows his interest by setting up a canoe club, or helping to introduce young people to the sport, or learning how to build canoes, is telling you a great deal about his general approach to life. He will be enthusiastic about the subject and only too happy to talk about it, so you are much more likely to find what you need to know by following this line than by asking endless questions about the fields of study he pursued at university. As the conductor of the orchestra, you are looking for what switches your chosen player on, because that is what you will need to know at some later stage.

Technical proficiency is obviously important – you cannot afford to take on board an engineer with a poor feel for his subject or who is ignorant of his responsibility in some specific areas. But with the right personal characteristics, technical knowledge can be topped up relatively easily and quickly. In any event, there is a constant reduction in the period of time before most technical people need re-training if their knowledge is to remain relevant. Many would now claim that the half-life of an electronics man is about four and a half years and even subjects which appear to be immutable, like mechanical engineering, have a half-life of only about a decade. Curiously few businessmen recognise this as an essential part of maintaining the fitness to perform of the individuals in their company. Time spent on refresher courses or even on single-day technical conferences is begrudged and looked upon as a 'jolly', rather than as an essential part of maintaining the capacity in which the individual was employed. People found reading technical journals at work are considered lazy or showing a lack of dedication to the cause. Indeed the specialist press is almost always the first area of cutting costs as a business becomes weaker. But of course none of these aids to maintaining the basic battery of knowledge is of the slightest use unless the individual is interested enough in the subject to wish to maintain his or her state-of-the-art effectiveness. When

59

checking and testing for technical capability what you are really doing is trying to assess the underlying degree of interest the individual has in the subject. It is useful to try to raise some sort of controversial area in the individual's speciality, to which there is not a right or wrong answer but the answers to which will show the degree of original thought, rather than the repetition of accepted dogma.

The starting point of any interview is to explain that the exercise is a two-way stretch. While you are interviewing the individual, the individual is endeavouring to make up his mind about the sort of people he is going to work with in the future. The consequences of a 'wrong' decision are equally dire for both of you: he will have wasted time, lost some confidence and may find it difficult to start again with someone else; you will have invested time, effort and money in a lost cause. An interview which saves both of you from such a mistake is just as successful as one which produces a future chief executive of the company. However, where an individual is judged unsuitable for your business, you at least owe it to him or her to give your views about the sort of company, business or job which might be more suitable for them. Candidates from university really have no idea what working within a company is like. They tend to have gained their views from older people or from academics who have seldom experienced a commercial life. When applying for a job with you, their reasons may be a mixture of sensible thinking and a path of least resistance

When I left the Royal Navy and applied for a job with ICI, I had three motivating reasons. The first, which I think was sound and would have withstood any examination, was that I believed the country faced economic problems in the future and I wanted to be in a basic rather than a luxury business. I had already made up my mind that I wanted to make things, as that seemed to be the most useful type of service I could render to my community. The other reasons would have been a great deal less convincing to an interviewer. Firstly, my brother-in-law, who had just joined the company, was full of enthusiasm about his experiences. This was entirely irrelevant, because he was a highly qualified engineer and I had no qualifications of any sort! Nevertheless, his pride in the company was a major factor in my seeking a job with them. Lastly, the company had recruited two other naval officers, both of whom had been close friends of mine and had worked in the same department of the intelligence division. They were full of enthusiasm for what they were doing and had found the contrast with the Royal Navy a marked improvement. Had I not happened to have a brother-in-law and two friends who had just joined ICI, I might still have applied to the company, but it was my tenuous personal connection which impelled me much more than the logic, even though I had thought the matter through carefully.

One needs to probe the motives of someone applying for a job within your particular business, but such probing will almost always evoke replies which, although they may well be true, border on obsequious flattery that yours is the best company in its field. If that reply is given, it is worth asking why; why has the candidate made such a statement and what does he believe is the basis of your competitive success? When interviewing candidates, it is absolutely essential to avoid leading questions. The worst of all are the sort to which there is only one acceptable answer – usually yes or no. 'Do you drink a lot of alcohol?' is unlikely to be answered with an enthusiastic (even if truthful) 'Yes!' and the question 'Are you good at taking the initiative?' is unlikely to be answered with a 'no' – no matter how qualified. The best sort of questions are of the 'what are your views on architecture?' type, to which there is no single correct answer but which may elicit clues to interests and background. The candidate should be given ample opportunity to ask questions about the company, or to ask your views or advice on any particular subject. Remember, however, that while the candidate is entitled to elicit information the object is for the interviewee to do the talking. If the candidate shows a certain interest in one of one's pet subjects, it is easy to fall into the trap of rabbiting on about yourself, your views, your experiences and so on. At the end of the interview you end up feeling warm, happy and well disposed to the candidate who has successfully interviewed you!

It is also important to try to build an emotional bridge with the candidate early on, no matter how slight. This may be that you know the town or village of his birth, or his current home, or his school, or you share an interest in ice hockey or tiddlywinks – anything to establish contact other than the formal position of interviewer and interviewee. Most candidates start in a highly nervous state. No matter how much you may explain that there is no such thing as success or failure in an interview, having to go back and admit to their friends or parents that they have not got the job represents a major failure. Most individuals, even those who have had a good deal of experience of jobs and interviews, look on interviews rather as a jockey at Aintree must view Becher's Brook. It is important to avoid squashing a candidate's confidence at any stage of the interview; the ideal is to get to the stage when he or she is less conscious of the formality and is sufficiently at ease to talk freely and openly about themselves, their interests, their motives and their ambitions. Even when candidates express views which are, in your opinion, stupid, a wise interviewer will merely comment on its being an interesting viewpoint.

The good interviewer will have done his or her homework and will approach the interview with some preliminary ideas, gleaned from the available paperwork. The application form should seek to draw out as much information as possible from the candidate; the sort of thing that will give you some starting clues about what to expect is initially the presentation of the application form. Is it well written and tidy, does it look as though the individual has not only thought his way through each answer but written it down before entering it on the form? Has he used the space available to best effect, or has he put in lots of unnecessary and extraneous words? Has he refused to be restricted by the size of the form when there is something he has wanted to say and written a separate note expatiating on some point he wants to make? What does the candidate seem to believe will be important to you as a company? Does he show signs of having investigated or read anything about the company?

The candidate who really wants the job will have put a great deal of thought into the completion of the form and will stress the points he believes relevant to the specific job and your particular business. What does the individual seem most proud of? In listing a range of outside interests, is there a balance between the physical and the artistic? Has the candidate undertaken a wide range of voluntary activities designed to expand their personality? Has he or she done the Duke of Edinburgh's Award? Do they appear to be religious or not? A well-designed and completed application form will produce a lot of information and some clear signs about what sort of person the interviewee is. But the interviewer should be prepared for surprises. Although I am constantly fascinated by the interviewing process and have spent much of my life meeting people in one context or another, I am always amazed how different the reality of an individual is from the mental picture drawn from written clues.

If the requirements of the job have been left as open as possible, so that people are not excluded on the basis of age, or some other mysterious qualification, you seldom receive an absolutely hopeless application. However, it is as well to be aware of the weaknesses of the written application as well as its strengths, and this is why it is vital to meet a candidate as well. A candidate can produce the most marvellous picture on paper which bears little or no resemblance to reality, or it can work the other way around. The individual will have taken time and pains about producing an application for a job, and it is easier to present a false picture in writing than it is in person. It is the veracity of that written picture and the weaknesses not exposed in it which are the key features you are looking for in the interviewing process. Time and again I find that the person who, on paper, seems ideally fitted for the job proves, in person, to have some major weakness or disadvantage, while the dark horse may come from a less appealing written application.

Most of the entirely hopeless candidates will be weeded out when the paperwork is first sifted. Although it is acceptable to have an assistant sort through and choose those who will be initially shortlisted, it is a good idea to get them to put two or three words on each rejected form to explain the reasons for rejection. This may clarify their thinking and benefit others who read the application forms, and the sensible interviewer will make sure that he has quickly checked the 'discards' – the ones who are not even going to get to the interview stage. It goes without saying that any applicant for a job must receive a reply from the company; more often than not this will be a simple statement that more suitable candidates have applied, but it should convey a bit more than that. The thing that infuriates people most of all, and does a company the most harm, is the absence of any reply whatsoever, but this is only marginally worse than an obvious standard response. Business people are busy, and most letters are of a fairly standard format, but it should not be beyond the wit of man to add a sentence or two to a standard

65

letter, which at least shows that you have read the application, that you are concerned about the individual and that you wish them success in the future. It is important that you do not contribute to reducing their self-confidence. I can not see that it does much harm to say that, while the individual's skill cannot be used in your company, you feel confident that they will do well in the future.

Of course the main clues that one is looking for in the application form are signs of achievement and striving for growth. There are a surprisingly large number of people who seem to be interview stars, but in practice are ineffectual. One can usually detect the glib braggart, but the sympathetically charming chap whose ideas gel with yours and who shows just enough individuality of expression is all too easy to fall for. What matters is what people have actually achieved, and sometimes the braggart is justified in his boasting by his accomplishments, whilst someone with the right chemistry may merely be a good talker with nothing to show. Your business needs doers and achievers – nice ideas or good motives are not in themselves enough. A careful reading of an individual's curriculum vitae should show signs of continual 'growth'; the jobs they move to and the tasks they have undertaken should all broaden their experience and increase their abilities. When short-listing candidates it is important to look for signs of progress through their lives, and to realise that a solid record of achievement is not signified merely by a list of job titles.

The curriculum vitae of experienced, mature people, their reasons for moving from one company to another are particularly important. The irony is that the individual who is constantly frustrated by not having enough head-room and who moves on to better himself may appear, purely from his C.V., remarkably similar to the individual who has consistently failed to achieve anything and has been nudged out of one company after another. It is the reasons for moving which are the key. Nobody should ever be blamed for one move when they found that the chemistry between themselves and their bosses did not work. However, four or five such moves are more likely to show that the candidate is one of the awkward squad.

Many companies go in for a whole battery of other selection aids, including psychological assessment and even graphology. Both these approaches are demonstrated as having something to offer in terms of insights into what makes people tick. I would have thought that my handwriting would have defeated any graphologist and yet blind readings of samples of my scrawl have been, in the view of my family, surprisingly accurate about some of my characteristics. I am not opposed to the use of any technique which helps the process, but the danger is that the more different evaluation techniques used the greater the temptation to duck one's responsibility for the ultimate choice and blame the 'technical assessment'. 'I thought he (or she) was fine but I could not accept him (or her) because of the graphology report', is a cop out. Such techniques are intended to provide clues for a different hypothesis which can then be followed, tested and developed, rather than a hurdle to be overcome. Particular danger signals to watch for in interviewing are strong emotional reactions based on positive or negative chemistry. We all have an instinctive view of an individual the moment we clap eyes on them – indeed meeting someone is a selective process during which we seek to categorise them according to our prejudices. The fact that a man wears a pony tail or a girl a nose ring is as irrelevant as whether they went to your old school or play golf or tennis at your club. If you find yourself feeling strongly for or against a candidate, that is the moment to redouble your efforts to check the reasons for your bias.

There are major differences between the selection procedures for new graduates and those for mature and experienced candidates. In the case of mature applicants they already have a track record of achievement and there are people you can talk to about them. You are less likely to benefit from a two-day selection procedure than in the case of the graduate. In my view it is worthwhile setting up a proper selection group for graduates, which should normally mean that the candidate has about three interviews. Interviewers should be chosen from, say, line managers with backgrounds of relevant responsibility and a selection specialist, who may be from any background but who has good analytical and selection skills, particularly with young people. As well as your interviewers having a mix of backgrounds, it is not a bad idea to have a mixed range of age and experience. In any event, it is important to ensure that all selectors are able to relate to younger people. Older people with families are often good in this area.

I also believe that something like six to eight graduates is the ideal number a selection board can deal with sensibly. You should be aiming for something like a 30 per cent success rate, so you should be looking to hire two or three of the candidates, but since quality is what you are essentially looking for, you should be prepared to be flexible. Top-quality people are always in short supply, and one does not get many opportunities to recruit. The policy in this regard needs careful thought; it is not sensible to have a prescriptive prohibition on recruiting a top-flight candidate when the opportunity occurs. The only circumstance under which it is worth forgoing the chance is if there is no available task for him or her to do. If someone joins you full of expectation and is put into a holding pattern, endlessly waiting to get stuck into a real job, they will quickly leave. Top organisations have a clear mental picture of the type of people they want and will recognise them quickly.

What is even more dangerous is to draft in inferior candidates because the initial selection has not turned up the quality of applicant you are seeking. If this happens once, it may be the luck of the draw, if it happens consistently you and your firm have a problem. Either in perception or in fact you are not competitive and the best young people do not want to know. If it is a question of the company reputation, this cannot be put right quickly; no amount of glossy advertising or slick PR will tempt the best people to trust you. There is no doubt that the best attract the best, and if you are consistent in your standards this is soon known. The undergraduate network will spread the news like lightning that a job with you is an accolade. Experience at Marks & Spencers, Shell or Ford has never harmed anyone's career prospects.

I believe that the whole board should take an interest in the graduate recruitment procedure. The chief executive, or at minimum a board member, should meet the group of candidates at the beginning and then spend a few minutes with each of them at the end. When the team have assembled and done the shortlisting, the ideal recruitment procedure should take an evening and a full day. The graduates should arrive the evening before and have an informal dinner with the selection group and the CEO or board member. Even though the evening is informal it will give you your first chance to see the candidates and how they interact with one another. Do they drink too much? Do they talk too much? Do they show off? Are they competitive, or are they calm and reflective? An informal evening can reveal a great deal. The following day each individual should be interviewed and then the whole group should be watched tackling specific practical tasks in sub-groups of three or four, in a competitive environment. These tasks will speedily show who are the natural leaders and will tell you a great deal about the way in which the individuals interact. At any time when they are not involved in interviews or practical tests, they should be given maximum opportunity to see the business and to meet individuals of their own age group who are working with you, so that they can find out as much as possible about the company and ask informed questions. Your best recruiting agents with graduates are young people who have recently joined you and who can say from first-hand experience what they like or dislike about the company. They can talk about the jobs they have been given and whether the company has lived up to their expectations. Young people feel more comfortable with their peers and are more likely to believe what they hear from them.

Many of these points apply equally strongly to interviewing the mature applicant, but there are important differences. The most obvious is that they have a history of performance in the world of work which should tell you how useful they are likely to be in your own set-up. The jobs they have filled, the things they are proud to have achieved and their reasons for moving on can all tell you a great deal about the person. Moreover, you will probably know someone with whom he or she has worked and a quick telephone call will fill in quite a bit of detail. Most people write references carefully to avoid damning the individual and will inevitably focus on the strengths. A direct question on the telephone about a candidate's weaknesses will usually achieve a direct response. I believe that it is sensible to make this sort of call before you interview the candidate, although most people seem to use this cross-check as a follow-up before they finally decide to offer a job. Remember, redundancy more often than not has nothing to do with the individual's performance and, if you can, it is worth asking questions about the criteria used for redundancy. It can be used to pay off old scores or get rid of the livelier people who have been agitating for change, so a bit of probing is in order. Surprisingly few companies use redundancy to cull the weak, although most will try to hang on to their best people. The roots of redundancy are more likely to derive from failures at the top of the company than with the hapless sufferers down the line.

Even though the task of selection is easier, there is more at stake with the mature candidate than with the young graduate. They will be joining you in a position of responsibility and can create a fair amount of havoc before you part company if you make a mistake. The amount of money at risk is also greater. The main aim of the interview with the mature candidate is to find out the type of person they are and their way of working, rather than their ability to do the task, which can be easily checked. The greatest danger is to be beguiled by the pleasant but ineffectual charmer or, on the other hand, to be put off the rough diamond whose qualities can be hidden by his hard edges. Social intercourse, a meal and drinks with a few future colleagues, can often be more revealing than a formal interview. In fact, with the mature person, the less formal the whole procedure the better.

Both types of applicant will talk about your company after their interview, but the mature applicant can have more impact in the outside world than the graduate. If he got the job, fine, but if he is not taken on there is a danger that he will speak in a derogatory way unless you have gone to some length to demonstrate fairness and concern for him. If refused, the interviewee must leave with his self-esteem and self-belief enhanced, but you must be careful how you do this. If true, it is helpful to say, 'We couldn't stretch you enough to utilise your potential', but if this is untrue you are building him up for a harder than necessary fall. Try to put yourself in their shoes: the poor devil who has been turned down for job after job and has been unemployed for two years is bound to be desperate and will often take anything, no matter how unsuitable. Your responsibility is greater in this case; you must ensure that you do not take him on out of misplaced kindness, only to set him up for another dismissal in the near future.

Interviewing is a specific skill and, like all managerial tasks, must be learnt and be reviewed regularly. Selection teams should spend time talking about their performance and striving to become more effective. It can be a good idea to ask one member of the team to prepare a critique of the interviews you have held, so that you can talk about them together. Since selection of the best people is the basis of your company's success it must be worth trying to do it better.

FIVE First Practice

When school leavers join your firm the pattern of their expectations about the organisation are formed within the first month or so. They will be at their most impressionable because they have very few standards of comparison. Cynicism has not yet set in and, above all, the individual has the sense that at last real life is starting and education is in the past. All the more important, therefore, to make sure that their first months in a new firm are not spent entirely in 'getting to know the ropes'. Many a good future employee gets a mistaken view about the expectations of their employer through being given a planned itinerary in which days or weeks are spent in each of the functional departments 'learning' what goes on. There is no sense of urgency and little follow-up to see what has been learnt. There is an overall impression that there are so many people and so little work to be done that it doesn't matter very much whether another pair of hands is working at the coal face or not. Such an approach is damaging because the new recruit is aching to get to work and have the opportunity to show his or her capabilities.

The opposite approach can be equally damaging. It is not helpful to be told to report at 9 o'clock on a Monday morning and to meet a harassed supervisor so torn between receiving myriad instructions from on high and making sure that those working are directing their efforts towards what is needed that there is little time for an extra task. A nod in a general direction and the encouraging words, 'that's where you'll be working – there's plenty to do, get on with it', hardly constitutes a helpful induction.

Introducing an employee to a new job requires as much thought on the part of the manager as any other aspect of his relationships with his employees. The first and most important point to make is that the start of a recruit's career is the direct responsibility of the line manager. In a great many companies and organisations it is left to the personnel department to make whatever arrangements are thought appropriate to get the individual there on time and to organise his or her introduction to the company. A priceless opportunity to reinforce the position and standing of the line manager is therefore lost. The impression is given that the well-being of the individual is the responsibility of an amorphous department rather than that of an individual. I believe that, even though the preparation and administrative work may well be done by a secretary, all the introductory experiences of a new recruit should appear to emanate from the manager who will be responsible for his work in the foreseeable future. The most helpful and human introduction to a new company takes the form of a letter from the line manager, which would read something like this:–

76

Dear Mr/Ms X,

I am delighted that you are joining my department and look forward to having the opportunity of working with you. I attach some background information about the company, and my department and its responsibilities. In addition, since you may not know the area where you will be working, I enclose a map and some more general information. I have asked Y, who joined us a year ago, to get in touch with you to ensure that any questions or queries you may have are answered. I have also asked Y to help you with any problems you may have regarding the finding of accommodation, and the initial problems associated with settling into a new area. I will be told if any matters require my intervention and, in the meantime, I look forward to seeing the two of you in my office at ten o'clock on the morning of 17 September. If you have any questions or problems that Y is not able to resolve on my behalf, please contact me direct.

The idea of having as a contact someone near one's own age is a helpful one, both to the manager and the new recruit. Y will recently have gone through the experience of joining the company straight from school or university and will therefore be aware of the terrors, concerns and pitfalls, most of which have perhaps been avoided. The beginner will feel less uncomfortable at revealing his relative ignorance to a contemporary than to his future manager.

At this stage most new recruits look upon their manager as

a curiously remote creature. They imagine that their relationship will be something like that they enjoyed at university with the head of department, rather than the direct and regular contact a working team should ideally enjoy with one and other. They will be particularly anxious to demonstrate their effectiveness, general confidence and savoir-faire. Whilst wishing to be treated as a fully fledged and experienced adult, they will still be suffering from the uncertainties which beset young people everywhere. A mentor can act as an excellent intermediary, and the experience of inducting a new recruit can be good for a man or woman who is a year or so into operating experience. The degree of perplexity and the concerns of people joining new communities are distressingly easy to forget. Everything is new; the area, the accommodation, the transport, the people, the job. Very few have confidence in their abilities to cope with any aspect of the many new tasks and experiences thrust upon them. For all these reasons it is a good idea to ask new recruits to join on a day when you know that adequate time can be allocated to introducing them to their new world. In addition to the obvious problems of accommodation, working hours, pay systems and conditions which have not been spelt out in the letter of appointment and so on, there are some critical instructions which they must be given before they start work of any sort.

Safety would always come top of my personal list. I believe that safety in a factory or work situation is an attitude of mind. Companies have an absolute obligation to remind their people of their individual obligations for their own safety and their collective responsibility for the safety not only of other employees but of the firm's customers and its neighbours. I believe that presentations on safety should be carried out even before an introduction to the work of the company. It should be demonstrated as being of pre-eminent importance in the eyes of the employer, and come before considerations of profit or anything else. I may be particularly sensitive in this area since I was accustomed to working in potentially hazardous conditions. Nevertheless almost every industrial or business process contains elements of risk and hazard, and it is a sign of a well run company that responsibilities in this area are reiterated and reinforced. Almost the first question I still ask when visiting any factory or firm is what the safety record is. Depressingly often, the answers reveal a cavalier attitude to something which should be the hallmark of a good employer.

After you have presented the safety policies of the company and given the necessary warnings to the new employees, the line manager has an ideal opportunity to present the aims and values of the company and the expectations which the firm has of its employees. Only when these preliminaries have been gone through is there any point in beginning to explain the job and make the various introductions which are appropriate. Again, it is important that the newcomer should be welcomed by the entire department and, if the opportunity occurs while making these introductions, it is a good idea to demonstrate that all members of the department are important. It is as essential to introduce new recruits to the cleaners as to the secretaries or section managers. If you leave young recruits to fend for themselves, they may have the nous to introduce themselves and make themselves known, but it is possible they will do so in a manner which alienates their new colleagues and starts them off on the wrong foot. It is the task of the mentor to make sure that the recruit meets everybody with whom there may be contact in the future and is given the opportunity of discussion with each of them.

Then on to the job. It is important that responsibilities should be passed as quickly as possible to people starting their career; the aim should be that the individual feels he or she is being stretched all the time for at least the first two or three years. They should feel that they are being asked to do more than they think they can achieve, but the tasks they are being given should not be beyond their ability. Just as in training and coaching a soccer team, or any process of physical fitness, one starts slowly and gradually but inexorably builds up, so it is with the world of work. Individuals must always feel the weight of responsibility. They should feel that help and advice are at hand but never that the job is being done for them. The task of the good coach is to help the performer to learn, not to produce precise instruction. Of course if it is a matter of the operating procedure for a piece of machinery demonstration will be necessary.

The balance between learning and doing is important. The man or woman will spend their careers doing both of these and, in an ideal world, he or she should start that way. A certain amount of responsibility should be given and an achievable target set, with a clear time-scale as to when it is required. At the same time the ground work for the next task should be prepared. Industrial and business life is never so simple and comfortable that you can do one thing at a time and then move sequentially on to the next at your own pace. Industrial and business life consists of endlessly struggling against an avalanche of things which need to be done and organising yourself so that you are always moving onwards. The very first lesson I was taught was that the job of any manager was one of constant improvement. This means not only improving one's own skills and achievements but helping those for whom one is responsible to develop their capabilities.

Nothing in the world of business is static: processes, products, cash, service to customers, should be changing for the better all the time. The pressures for change in this modern world never stop and there is never a perfect business – simply one which is temporarily better than its competitors. There is a very big difference between this and the academic background your young recruit has just come from. There it was believed that there was a clear answer to every question. The task was to learn the answers and produce them as required. In business there is never one single answer, moreover, what appears to be a perfect answer today is unlikely to be a perfect answer in a month's or a year's time. This change, from a world of apparent absolutes to one of change and improvement, is very difficult to bridge. The attitudes involved in striving for improvement are not ones

81

inculcated during most people's schooling. These attitudes are learnt in the pursuit of sport or physical fitness, but are not usually seen as key attitudinal elements in the pursuit of a career. The ability to look critically at everything within one's field of responsibility and to puzzle non-stop at the things which you believe could be improved, is extremely difficult to achieve. Young people who join companies think they are being employed to 'supervise', 'oversee' or 'take decisions'. The idea that they are the prime instrument of change and that the pace, scale and goal of change is their main area of responsibility is not easily or quickly understood.

One of my first jobs in my industrial career was to study the operation of an incinerator. I quickly realised that the major problem was the lack of any systematic way of feeding the mix of materials into the furnace, and rushed back to announce my assessment to my boss. Far from being congratulated, I was told to go back and do a proper job. My boss was right; there was much more to be learnt about the characteristics of the various combinations of feeds and a lot more improvement to be achieved. The induction of a beginner involves questioning what is being done and pointing out where things could have been done better, while still supporting their confidence, so that the individual doesn't feel that what he does will never be satisfactory. People learn fastest when there is a careful balance between praise (for effort) and expectations (for higher achievement). A regime of exhortation for more and better, coupled with apparent disregard for the efforts put in or sacrifices made

82

by the individual, is a dispiriting one to work under, even if you believe that the end result will be worthwhile. Young people in particular need encouragement and to have their self-esteem and self-belief reinforced. This is more likely to be achieved by statements like, 'That's a jolly good effort, but don't you think it could have been done a little better if we did this, or that, or the other'. The regime can get a little harsher as confidence is built up, but the initial balance needs to be weighted more towards encouragement than will be the case at later stages in their development. The aim should be for the new recruit to 'hit the ground running'. The luxury of idle time should not be given and, from the first, a pretty spanking pace should be set to get the new starter up to speed with the expectations of the company as a whole.

If you have got the pacing right there should not be too much time or energy left to pursue a hectic social life in the first few weeks. Nevertheless it is important to remember that no one works for a company every minute of every day. A balanced life is as important for a young person starting a job as it is in later life. The irony of business life is that, as a broad generalisation, the people at the top work very long hours indeed and give of themselves unstintingly, while those at the bottom follow a more relaxed and less demanding lifestyle. While this still happens in many companies, the aim should be to try to get the strain more equalised. New recruits should look back on their first months as having been very hard work, during which they were concerned about their ability to carry the level of responsibility apparently thrust upon them. In a well-organised set up the reality will be that someone will be keeping a careful eye on the workload and responsibilities, but it is important that this should not be realised. Nor should you intervene until the very last moment. Too much checking or early intervention removes the feeling of responsibility and delays the growth of the well-rounded, self-motivated manager, which is the object of the exercise. It is equally important to demonstrate at an early stage that your young people are not just new slaves to be fed to the inexorable machines but people who can and should make a difference. I now recognise that my first two years in ICI were characterised by my being given the difficult jobs, which in some cases others had failed. The increase in my self-confidence when I managed to resolve a long standing problem was very real and as my self-confidence grew so it became possible for me to tackle ever more difficult tasks.

Among the mentor's other responsibilities should be to find out what the recruit's interests and hobbies are and to make sure that he knows of local opportunities for following them, be they sailing, folk-dancing or pub-crawling. The manager responsible should initially aim to spend a bit of time with the new employee every week. It does not have to be a tremendously detailed review of the week's work, but fifteen minutes or so of talking about what has happened, what has been achieved and what are the difficulties will cement the relationship and give a clear view of the progress which is being made to enable the manager to tighten or loosen the pressure as appropriate. It might be a good idea

84

for the manager to invite the new recruit to his home or to a meal in a pub or restaurant after about six weeks in the job, and it can be helpful for people further up the line to have the opportunity to meet him socially after he has been with the company for a few months. As a chairman of a large company, I was always anxious to meet the young people who had joined within the previous few months. Such meetings gave me the opportunity to reinforce the value system of the company, as well as to check the calibre and quality of new recruits. I also very often came away with a fresh and valuable viewpoint on how the company looked from the bottom up. Companies accept the absurdities which have grown in them over a period of time and seldom give rise to comment from those who have grown with them. The new recruit, who was not involved in the development of some of the more curious practices, frequently has a different viewpoint which can shed a valuable light on some of the odder developments. These innocent comments can often lead one to question why things are done in certain ways, which encourages the important aim of improving and changing what is out of date.

There are many different views about the role of social life within a company or organisation. I have never been one of those people who think that companies gain by ensuring that every moment is spent in a company environment. Unfortunately, this happens all too easily if you are the dominant employer in an area and if the habits and customs of your company are patriarchal, so that the best club, school

85

and sports ground are run by your company. Fortunately, modern attitudes and the pressures of economic necessity, mean that this is less likely to be the case now. Nevertheless there is a happy medium. Your young people have mostly come from climates where 'everything' was provided within their university or college of further education. It is helpful to see that they have a reasonable level of organised social welcome, but this should stop a long way short of telling them the 'right' golf club to join or which restaurants are appropriate for which grades of management, for example. I mean these comments in all seriousness, since I have known firms which have set out to delineate their employees' lifestyles in just such degrees of intrusive detail. I remember being repelled by the advice of a well-meaning superior who told me in all seriousness that my future career would be affected by my social activities. I was encouraged by him to join the golf club and to attend the annual social ball. So incensed was I that I resolved to do neither and thus lost the chance of taking part in a harmless and enjoyable sport. Your employees will decide for themselves what levels of interaction they wish to enjoy outside normal business activities. Inevitably you will find some of them heading towards the same sorts of clubs, bars and activities and, in itself, this is not a bad thing, but best generated by the people themselves.

Many companies believe in elaborate job descriptions which define the scope, responsibilities, powers and even, in many cases, the ways of doing the job. I do not think this is the best way to 'grow' people. Not only does it restrict individual initiative but it produces a lack of flexibility in the organisation, which can be fatal. It is important that newcomers are helped to realise the freedom they have about how they do things, rather than concentrating on the restrictions. I believe that what is required in most companies is an accurate description of the responsibility of the job – what the objective of the job is and what it has to achieve. Clearly there must be some delineation of limits of authority; – you cannot, for instance, allow the newcomer to commit large sums of money without consultation with more experienced members of staff. But it is important that if restrictions are placed upon their freedom of action they should be coached that they do not represent excuses for inaction or restrict the imagination brought to bear on the aim they have been given. The more that the openness of opportunity is emphasised, the more you will teach young people the limitations of what can be done and the more you make them look to the broader aspects of business and their role within it.

There are very few tasks in business which can be carried out by one person on his or her own. They will almost always be responsible for some people below them, and for collaborating and working with people in other departments and other fields of activity. The job description should make it clear where the primary responsibility for achievement lies, but should also make clear that the goal must be reached with the help and collaboration of other departments, suppliers, customers and, if necessary, outside organisations. The newcomer should be encouraged to think as broadly and to consult as widely as possible. One of the things that he or she has probably brought with them from further education is the understanding of where to seek knowledge, although they may have less understanding of how to apply it. The point must be made regularly that the individual will be judged by achievements rather than by the way that achievement was reached. At the same time it must be made clear that business relies on ongoing relationships, and it is important that in the process of achieving the goal set by the company people should be involved and supportive rather than antagonised, because their help will inevitably be needed on future occasions. These are lessons which can only be learnt in practice and through continual gentle coaching. Questions such as, 'What does so and so think about it?', 'Have you looked to see what the competitors are doing?', or 'What would your customers think about this approach?', can all direct attention outside the department or the company, and it is essential that new starters should learn to think in these broader terms.

Young people often believe that the road ahead lies in satisfying their boss, or achieving good marks in a test. They do not so readily understand that they are being tested by everyone they are now in contact with, be they subordinates, peers or others in commercial relationship with them. Both the manager and the mentor should initially set limited and specific tasks and explain why the task has been chosen and how it relates to the overall responsibility for the job. It is important for the manager to be prepared to give quite basic and seemingly almost simplistic help and advice. All too often the beginner finds it hard even to work out the appropriate starting point to achieve required goals. But here, too, it is important that the newcomer should be guided rather than instructed. Suggestions such as, 'There seem to me to be three potential starting points for this task. What do you think about them and which do you think would be the most effective in moving you towards your ultimate goal?' are more useful than saying, 'In the next three weeks I want you to have studied this and achieved that'. After all, there is never a single unique action that has to be undertaken at a specific moment. There are umpteen ways to reach the goal and, even at this very early stage of business, it is worth putting the emphasis on getting the commitment of the newcomer to the particular task chosen. Time and effort must not be wasted on something which has no relevance to the long term responsibility set. Young people easily confuse activity with achievement and will often think that the most important thing is to show that they are active and working hard. Of course you would expect them to be doing so and, indeed, provided the field of responsibility has been set broadly enough, there is no excuse for them not doing so. But the key to their first job is to enable them to learn that successful application to a part of the problem will succeed in shifting the whole problem along. For example, the overall task may well be to reduce the cost of production by the maximum possible during the coming year. The initial task to achieve this could well be to analyse total costs of production under different headings and to make a guess what savings might be possible under each heading. From this might come specific approaches to the potential savings identified in all the various areas, be it the elimination of a production step, the reduction of cost on a component, the redesign of the total operation or lay-out, a better computer control system, or whatever. In business or industry jobs always involve breaking down large objectives into specific fields where action can be taken, and inevitably a newcomer will not have the clarity of approach of an experienced operator.

You have to make a choice about the first task you give your new recruit. This can either be within the minimum field of activity, making clear what the relevance to the whole is and stating clearly which other functions, managers and departments will probably have to be asked for help, or you can set a broader problem and focus in from that to the specific actions that should be undertaken. The time to learn these key lessons is from the very start of one's business career. The very first instruction which I was given in business was that my job was to find better and cheaper ways of producing more from less. I was then given a series of relatively small, self-standing jobs where I was expected to apply this approach. Although it is important to keep the newcomer focused on carrying out the task in hand, it can also be helpful to encourage study of some other aspect of activity perceived as being necessary to the overall achievement of the business goal. Obviously it is better if the impetus for doing this comes from the novice himself. I remember being immensely impressed by a young trainee commercial manager who, off his own bat, came to the conclusion that he needed to learn a particular foreign language to be able to do his job properly and, without invoking the company's help, enrolled in an evening class. It seemed to me that his preparedness to make that sort of investment in himself to be more able to compete in his field of responsibilities was admirable. If the ideas are not forthcoming it is far better to lead gently by persistent questioning than to state baldly that you require Spanish to be learnt and have arranged a start next week.

This interaction between learning, experience and ownership of a problem are the components which the manager, coach and mentor must try to bring into balance if the newcomer is to start with the right approach and outlook. Beginners should not be saved persistently from making mistakes. You cannot of course afford major errors which are going to cost the company or its customers large sums of money, but people frequently learn more from their mistakes than from their successes. The judgement about how far one should allow a newcomer to continue on the wrong path is a difficult one. It is almost always better to wait until he or she realises that their path is not going to lead in the desired direction. Better by far to help the newcomers to dig themselves out of the pits they have jumped into with such good intentions, than to yank them out and tell them to start again.

Initially, you will have to be prepared to spend a good deal of time coaching and overseeing the beginner, but it is important that he should still feel that he is steering his own boat. If he feels that every step taken is being monitored the conclusion will be drawn that no responsibility is his. The

good manager will ensure that his 'guiding hand' is as unob-
trusive as possible and rely on his scheduled weekly chats
to produce the guidance required. The most fatal mistake
with young people is to take the problem away from them;
frequently they get completely lost and say bluntly that they
do not know what to do next or where to go from where
they are. This is a time for patient listening and careful
questioning, and on no account must you tell them what to
do. To allow them to work out their own solution it is
worth nudging them to come up with a number of possible
solutions and saying 'Come back this afternoon or tomorrow
morning when you have thought about these and tell me
how you intend to go ahead then'. When they have said
what they do intend to do, you should give encouragement
rather than an alternative solution. If the route they are
taking is one which will lead them into trouble, ask the
relevant questions again. 'What do you think the effect of
that will be on Mr X, or the costs of Y, or customer Z?'
Because the employee is inexperienced he or she will often
not have thought of these possible repercussions and your
task is to broaden horizons and perspectives while the man
or woman is learning about your business.

The most dangerous situation is one in which newcomers
not only become lost but actually give up, where they
become so overwhelmed by the problems that they are
incapable of further constructive action. If you see signs of
this, it is vital to move in quickly, but without taking the
problem away. Questions such as 'How are you getting on?',
'What are you doing now?', 'Why do you think that will

work?', 'What are the other things you could do?', are all the staple fare of the manager. At the same time the manager and the mentor will be sitting down and discussing the new recruit's progress and in many cases suggestions can come via the mentor more easily than from the manager. The process is helpful to the mentor, the newcomer and the business as a whole, but the mentor must also be cautioned against the removal of problems and responsibilities from the new recruit. From the very beginning he or she must feel that the responsibility for the achievement of the goal set rests upon his or her actions alone. It will be helpful if the individual can be brought gently to understand that this will be the pattern of the rest of his or her working life.

six The Coach

It is at this early stage that the whole pattern of the individual's career and his potential future in the company is decided but not by any carefully detailed plan. I have never met a manager who was taught the art of managing and 'growing' an individual – largely because the skill of developing and coaching and growing latent talent is personal. The manager and the subordinate have the usual differences and idiosyncrasies, so what works with one person or at one time will not do so at another. We know that our own attitudes vary enormously from day to day, dependent on a host of inter-related factors: our health, a self-inflicted hangover, our confidence in our relationships with others, whether we left home in a state of tension, and so on. All these vary for each of us every day, and even at different times of the day. Because management is an interaction between two people, two more or less random mental and physical conditions are interacting. It is perhaps easier to see this in the context of our relationships with our wives, husbands or children. We know, even in the much safer and less exacting confines of our homes, how difficult and

95

complex these are; they can be sustained only by our commitment to each other and our belief in the binding institutions of marriage and parenthood.

It is obvious that it is far more difficult to develop and sustain relationships in the world of work. Firstly, there is no permanence about the relationship. Either the manager or the subordinate may be moved to other duties at any time – indeed they may never meet again in a professional sense, and there is therefore no underlying feeling that the repercussions may have to be lived with in years to come. Secondly, there is commitment to the enterprise. Although virtually nobody works purely for the sake of the money, the days have long gone when the mere possession of a job meant that one had metaphorically committed the rest of one's life to that firm or task. Mostly we look on the job we have been given as a stepping-stone to the achievement of a wider career objective – for example we may have joined a particular firm to gain experience in a specific field which will enable us to have a greater 'market value' elsewhere. At the least we do not envisage working for the same firm or doing the same task for the rest of our working lives, and nor should we. The basis of a modern business career is that one should be growing and becoming able to cope with ever more complex challenges. The tasks we are involved in today enable us to carry out more ambitious, and satisfying jobs in the future. This is where the analogy with the orchestra really comes in to play. Next week or next year we will be playing different, probably more difficult, music to a different audience, but the experience we have gained in this performance will allow us to play more confidently in the future. The common ground between the two experiences will be the proficiency and skill with which we play our individual instrument, our ability to relate to the other instruments in the orchestra and how we cope with a different conductor, who may have his own interpretation of the same piece of music, in order to produce a better performance.

The art of managing individuals, and it is an art, does not come easily. Nor does it come without work, commitment and study. This attempt at continual improvement applies both to the generalities of managing large numbers of people and to the specifics of managing and relating to one individual. It is quite extraordinary that some managers believe they can obtain the best from their people on the basis of seeing them perhaps for an hour once a year and keeping a casual eye on their output. Many people think that a manager's responsibilities comprise little more than an annual appraisal meeting and an occasional jog of the memory that it is X who is responsible for Y. Nothing could be further from the truth, and those who manage in this way reap the results of their lack of care.

Managing an individual is more akin to bringing up a child, or the teacher's relationship to a pupil at school: the task is never-ending. While nothing inhibits the growth of an individual more than constant correction and supervision, the good manager should be aware of his subordinate's thoughts, attitudes and problems as well as his tasks. The first essence of managing an individual is to be mentally attuned to his thoughts and emotions and to understand his perceptions of his capabilities, which will vary both from reality and from your personal beliefs as to what he can do. The manager's greatest weapon is self-belief and the conviction that he or she can achieve the objective set. This should not be confused with arrogance. The good manager is acutely aware of personal shortcomings and knows where or when he will need assistance, advice or the involvement of experts or others to accomplish the task ahead. But underlying everything must be a personal commitment to the achievement of the task and this commitment is not possible unless the manager believes not only that he can ensure the task is accomplished but that he can do it better than others. This self-belief can only be built up through a record of achievement, because it takes a very particular kind of individual to return again and again to a task at which they have never had any success, in the stubborn determination that ultimately they will succeed. There are such individuals, who seem to derive added will for the fight from failure, but most of us require to win more often than we lose. Although some degree of failure is inevitable, it is important that it should be seen as an opportunity to do better next time and a brave attempt at something beyond our existing capability, but which in time will succeed.

Since the task of the manager is to increase the aspirations and capabilities of his subordinate he has a great responsibility for setting the pace of learning and for ensuring that the balance between success and failure is optimal. Setting individuals to do tasks easily within their competence results in over-confidence and can lead to a lackadaisical approach to work and the belief that failure is impossible. If the task is made too difficult, the individual is likely to become discouraged and begin to doubt his or her abilities. They then enter a downward spiral where they become incapable of carrying out jobs which are well within their capabilities. Judging the balance is very much a matter of individual discretion: there is a very narrow line between success and failure. However, most managers err on the side of too little challenge rather than of asking too much. A moment's reflection about the conditions under which one works best oneself will show that the best performance is achieved by the combination of an objective a little further away than one thinks one can achieve combined with relentless expectation from above that one will achieve it.

It is important to make it very difficult for someone to pass their responsibility up the line to their superior. The task that is ours must remain ours and, while we are entitled to look for advice, encouragement or warning from our manager, we are not entitled to decide that the problem is too difficult for us and give it back. The difficulty is that many managers love to demonstrate their abilities by removing responsibilities from their subordinates. After all, you were promoted because you could do the job of the subordinate and presumably as well or better than others. What better opportunity to lead by example than to tell your subordinate exactly what he or she should do? Such actions are often fatal. By the simple action of taking the task away, you have assumed the commitment and ownership of the assignment. You have taken the responsibility away and the carrying out of that responsibility is the process by which the individual grows. It may be satisfying for you to demonstrate how easily you can do what your appointee is struggling with, but it doesn't help him. What is being sought is not a carbon copy of you five years ago (which was probably the last time you did the task), but to see the application of a fresh mind, younger than yours, more up to date with technological and other developments, tackling a similar sort of responsibility in a personal and different way. This is the way companies and individuals make progress; the changes in attitude and skill of each successive generation enable progress to be made. Business is a race to change and improve faster than your competitors. Above all it is a mental race, not just of knowledge, but of the capability, determination, originality and sensitivity of your people against their competitors. It will be won only by firms which embrace and involve the full range of abilities of all the people in the company.

One of the tools most managers use at some point is to carry a notebook with them so that they can note, on a chronological basis, ideas, actions and facts from the plethora of meetings and interactions they have each day. If you are trying to coach only a small number of subordinates, a form of diary will be quite enough to enable you to check on the last tasks that related to your subordinate. However, if you are trying to coach a number of people, it may be worthwhile having a separate notebook for each individual. In advocating this sort of approach I do not mean that one

100

should painstakingly record every conversation. But it is well worth noting how often you have spoken to your subordinate about the tasks he has in hand and perhaps jotting down one or two factual numbers about the progress being achieved. If one is trying to coach a number of people, it is easy to allow the periods between 'checking times', when you drop in on an individual, to lengthen and lengthen. This is particularly the case when the individual seems to be working well and has plenty of confidence. When the day comes that he overreaches or feels he is getting lost, you will be lucky if your relationship with him is such that he will come to you to talk about where he is. It is more likely that he will go on until he has made an avoidable error, which you would perhaps have been able to forestall if you had stayed in touch.

A lot of play has been made in recent years of the technique of management by walking about. This is not so much a technique as the normal way managers should manage. During most of my business life I have tried to make it a practice to see at some time during the day, everybody for whom I was responsible. 'Seeing' does not necessarily involve exchanging conversation, apart from saying 'Good morning' or 'How are you?'. What it does mean is having actually visited the individual at his place of work and got some idea of what was going on. An experienced manager walking about can detect whether trouble is looming, whether somebody is not pulling on the oars or has lost control of his boat and is being carried away by the rapids.

101

The more this is done as a routine, the less importance individuals attach to a visit from the boss, and the more likely you are to pick up early warnings in good time, so that a gentle word of advice may be enough to persuade your subordinate to re-examine the way he is working. This word of advice should not involve giving the answer as you see it. One must ask open-ended questions and never lead to specific conclusions except in the most subtle manner. People value more what they learn for themselves and it is the lessons one teaches oneself that endure. A manager should aim to stimulate the wish to learn, encourage the learning process and ensure that the means of learning are available. The task of the coach is not to do the sums and produce the solutions, but to enable the subordinate to do the sums and produce solutions of his own.

Of course, one of the reasons why managers find this approach so difficult is that every manager carries the full responsibility for the performance of those below him, and it is therefore difficult to watch an inexperienced young person tackling a task in a way which is totally different from yours. I remember many years ago having a fierce argument with a new young manager when a major reorganisation was necessary for the lay-out of part of our enormous stores. I believed the best way of tackling the problem was the way I had dealt with a similar one only two years earlier. At that time I had closed a section at a time and 'blitzed' it over a period of days, but my young starter was determined to do the job without shutting down anything at all. I didn't think it was possible and believed that the job would never be finished. I was out of date. The demand for service from each section had grown to such an extent that shutting down would have created more chaos than the alternative. I eventually shut up, and told him to do it his way – but woe betide him if he failed to meet our agreed time table. Needless to say, he romped home and I gladly acknowledged that he had been right. It is only by reminding ourselves that times have changed, that in business there is always more than one way of doing a task and by being clear that the primary aim is that the ownership of the problem remains firmly in the young person's grasp, that we can have the courage to allow our subordinates to grow. Of course, the truth is that if we do not allow them to grow, we are stopping progress, and will fail in the discharge of our broader responsibilities because our section or department is stuck in a timewarp.

Having and projecting belief in the capability of your subordinates is a character-testing part of the role of manager, and a part in which all too many of us fail. Encouragement is of the greatest possible importance – on a scale of sticks and carrots, there should be about ten carrots to every stick, and the carrots should be large and obvious while the sticks should be small. If you have got the scale of the task right, so that your subordinate feels challenged by what you have asked them to do, your job is to reinforce their belief that they can do it by the projection of your own confidence. This confidence has to be projected irrespective of whether you truly feel it.

Frequently you will find that the subordinate who owns

103

the problem will succeed in ways quite different from those you thought would have worked, and in circumstances which you thought would lead to disaster. The essence of 'growing' people is this combination of demand for performance, encouragement in doing the task and space or head-room to perform, and this is where communication between the manager and subordinate is so important. It is only if you are in touch with what is going on that you can judge whether to provide another small carrot, or whether to make observations such as, 'There are six or seven different ways of tackling this task, why did you choose this one?', or words of warning such as, 'Good luck, I hope this works out, but do watch the so and so'. These forms of coaching are better done on the run and on the subordinate's territory, than in a weekly progress chat in the manager's office. You still need the progress chats and perhaps to note down each week where you think the task has got to, but the difficulty with a formal weekly progress meeting is that it can become a ritual. It has its uses as a spur to action, since the subordinate will know that he has to report his progress to his manager every week – and there had better be some progress. On the other hand, it can rapidly turn into a game where the subordinate hoards one or two achievements in case his project hits the doldrums the following week. I believe that regular progress chasing, coupled with the discipline of a weekly note about how things are moving is the best way of combining head-room with sensible supervision.

A point which good coaches often question themselves about is consistency of approach. You may not feel that you are the world's greatest authority on the task that you have set your subordinate, but from his point of view you represent his only access to experience and knowledge, as well as being the judge and jury of his performance. If he is to learn, or more accurately if he is to teach himself how to do the task, he needs to feel that his manager is consistent in his approach. As well as enabling your new team member actually to discharge his responsibilities, you are trying to develop in him a philosophy of management and an approach which will enable him, over a period of time, to develop without coaching. One of your tasks is to impart your beliefs and the values which guide you in your approach to business. Questioning whether we can't do a bit better, or if this is the best we can possibly achieve, involve an attitude to improvement which is part of such a value system. The willingness to examine any apparent constraint and to consider whether there is any absolute except the necessity for achievement, produces the flexibility of approach and mind which is likely to bring the best out in young people.

One of the primary jobs of the managerial coach is to overcome some of the rigidities of our education system. The concept that there are problems for which there may be no absolute solution, or that a quick and workable solution may be adequate is difficult for young people to comprehend. One of the slogans I have always believed appropriate in business is that 'the best is the enemy of the good'. There are a number of reasons why I feel that this is true. Firstly, the pursuit of the perfectionist solution takes too long, and time and timeliness are the essence of business. By the time you have worked out a perfect solution, it has often been overtaken by events and is irrelevant. Secondly, the perfection you are seeking exists in your mind and may not meet your customer's needs. Your 'best' solution may not be appreciated at all; and it certainly will not be if it is too late. It is even more difficult to get across the concept that while there may be a 'best' solution at present, that solution is unlikely to be valid tomorrow, or in a year's time. Understanding of the flexibility required in business is difficult for young people to learn because it involves taking responsibility in a different way, and says that their approach to learning has to be different. Their long years of education have taught them that learning is a matter of memorising facts and of being able to assemble those facts in different ways. Facts are of the greatest importance in business, but they are simply clues and indicators to courses of action and need rigorous checking, because all too often an accepted fact is the constraint which prevents progress or action. It is only when the fact is tested, quite often to destruction, that the constraint is removed and progress and action can ensue. These are difficult concepts for young people to assimilate and particularly difficult if they excelled academically. The dichotomy is that people need both abilities: they need the academic background and understanding of their subject, but it has to be coupled with flexibility of mind and the willingness to challenge, which is the basis of good business sense.

As I have said, everything achieved in business is achieved with or through people. Be they customers, suppliers, subordinates or superiors it is the 'managing' of this cat's cradle of relationships, while still maintaining speed of progress, that is the task of the manager. A major part of the coach's job is to keep the attention of the subordinate on the impact of his task on the views and feelings of those whom he in turn is trying to lead, or the customers, suppliers or other departments involved in his objective. It is difficult for young people accustomed to a clear hierarchical set up to understand that it is their responsibility to manage this complex array of relationships. After all, it is as much the responsibility of the subordinate to manage his manager as of the manager to manage his subordinate. All too often young people believe in the military approach to organisation. They therefore expect that when they are given the responsibility for carrying out a particular task they are also given the power to command the support of all those involved. I remember when I was given the responsibility of trying to sort out the labour problems on the Wilton site asking for, and being refused, line responsibility for the senior managers of the divisions operating on the site. I thought the refusal unreasonable, but the divisions were, (even though a part of ICI as a whole) my customers. It was up to me to persuade them rather than to instruct. Although the responsibility and objective given to your subordinate should be clear to everybody involved, the task will be accomplished only by the freely given collaboration of a large number of people, all with different skills and from different departments.

Ultimately, every individual in an organisation, even one

closely controlled, has two key areas of freedom – his attitudes and his use of work time. These cannot be proscribed
by authority, and people will give their support to a project
only if they are convinced that it is worthwhile. It is the
job of the junior manager to persuade those involved to
collaborate and assist. In almost every case this is made
more difficult because collaboration will involve some trade
off or diminution in the technical purity of what they are
seeking to achieve in the interests of speed or profit.

It is noticeable that in practically all cases where progress
is being sought in one department, adjustments in other
parts of the organisation are necessary if headway is to be
achieved. It is surprising how often improvements in the
production line can only be achieved if the design department are prepared to redesign, the sales department to consider a change in specification, the distribution department
to change their methods of delivery, or the suppliers the
nature of the item they supply. In almost all these cases
such interactions are achievable only by individuals being
prepared to compromise on their personal objectives to make
the end result better. The job of the young manager is to
understand this and to be willing to 'give up' a part of his
ambition to help others. This is a far cry from the certainties
of a black-and-white instruction coming from 'God' and a
feeling that unquestioning and mindless obedience is the
only requirement. The task of young people is to become
involved and to understand the complexities of the total
business situation in order to make their contribution. Yet
again this responsibility flies in the face of their previous

training: compromise of the part for the better progress of the whole is not an academic concept and does not arise easily from the lessons of school and higher education.

Even though one of the sure signs of a good manager is the ability to develop the abilities of his or her subordinates, few bosses value this as highly as the achievement of the main business objective. If the people in our businesses are to be used to the maximum, this attitude to managerial responsibility must be changed at all levels of the organisation. It is important that when coaching the new young manager their responsibility for coaching in turn should be made apparent to them. This may seem difficult for a young person who has little experience, since people invariably confuse coaching with teaching. Coaching involves the development of the whole person and even the youngest and newest raw recruit can do something in these areas. In particular, the beginner can be taught that, while ultimate responsibility cannot be evaded, it can be exercised only by encouraging subordinates and showing trust in them. No manager can control every detail, but no good manager can pass the blame for failure down the line. This lesson is taught early on in the Services, but in business the buck is often passed further and further away from the boss who had responsibility in the first place. If the subordinate fails, he or she was badly chosen or badly briefed or badly supported or badly trained and whose fault is this? This lesson can most easily be learnt at the beginning of one's business career, because one is then aware that the people one is responsible for know better than you how to do their

109

particular jobs – indeed your problem is often what you can possibly bring to the party. The 'what' that you can bring is the willingness to listen and to understand, together with the application of a new and inquiring mind to the practices which have prevailed for so long in your organisation. You can also bring a sense of your own personal values, integrity and commitment to the business objective as a whole.

Do not fall into the trap of judging beginners purely on their level of achievement. The way they do things is valid and there is a major opportunity to teach young people the importance of analysing this, combined with interpersonal relationships, at the very beginning of their careers. The good manager thinks about how they do things and, while this is an abstract concept, the management of how things are done is a concrete one. Among the lead questions that should be put to young people are: What are you going to do next? What is the next step? How are you going to get the ownership of this problem transferred to X,Y or Z? How are you going to manage the meeting that you are holding next week? What are the objectives of the discussion you are holding on Tuesday? All these force attention to the process of carrying out the work, as well as the ultimate achievement. Much can be taught by questioning whether the objectives of the meeting with so and so were achieved and, if they weren't, the reasons why they failed. What went wrong at the meeting? At what stage was it apparent that you couldn't achieve the objective? Why do you think X acted in the way he did? As well as showing a proper degree of interest and concern in the work and concerns of your

110

subordinate, questions of this type inexorably teach the approach to work that you are seeking to instil. Attention to the development of process skills at this stage will pay off handsomely as your subordinate becomes more and more able to undertake difficult tasks through the support, freely given, of other people. There are a number of specific gimmicks to managing process which can be taught and it may be that there will be areas of experience or knowledge which need filling in by more formal training than can be given by coaching on the run.

I shall be discussing training in the next chapter. While training is an essential part of coaching, it is not the end objective of the developmental process. Most of the development of people is carried out while they are at work and is a combination of the tasks and responsibilities they are given, together with the demands placed upon them. The term 'on the job training' is one I abhor, because it generally implies that people will pick things up as they go along. The developmental responsibility of the coach-manager is much broader than that, it is to ensure that the work processes your subordinate is dealing with contribute to the development of skills and managerial ability. This is no mean task. It may well be that the scope for developing the particular skills you believe your subordinate requires are not easily encompassed within the field of responsibility he or she has been given. The good manager will therefore always be looking for opportunities to give additional tasks to his subordinate which will develop such skills or knowledge.

I well remember in my early days in ICI working for a boss who took his responsibilities for developing his subordinates very seriously indeed. I was amazed at the working parties he saw fit to have me to deal with. They were often subjects far outside my field of responsibility at the time (when I happened to be manager of the supply department). Such extraneous tasks gave me the opportunity to learn about other fields of activity in the complex world in which I was operating, and to work with people from different departments who approached problems in different ways and saw practical difficulties of which I had no inkling.

Besides constantly stretching the individual by asking him to perform more than he thinks he can, the tasks given should also seek to fill the gaps in his experience. When a young manager first joins an organisation it is unlikely that he will have any real experience of the complexities of the operation. This is particularly true in large organisations, where matters become highly specialised. The problems of supply or distribution, sales, research, development or information technology are dealt with by separate departments which seem to have lives of their own. One of the great advantages of the small organisation is that all these specialities are dealt with by the small group of people who are managing the whole outfit. They may well buy in specialist services needed, but even in the act of buying they have to understand a great deal more about what they need and expect and the contribution that, for example, information technology can bring to the business as a whole. In large organisations this balance of view across all the fields of specialisation can only come from the top. Despite this, every individual down the line has to learn to work with other departments and to involve and utilise them if they are to achieve the business objectives they have been set. Today it is almost impossible to carry out any research project without the active involvement of information technology, and the influence of accountancy and cost accounting should be felt in every area of the business. It is as necessary for the young manager to understand the mechanics of such activities as the dynamics of their management. To achieve a trade-off between the various departments for the best possible performance of the whole, there has to be an understanding at every level of the pressures, ambitions and objectives of the entire company.

A view which is gaining increasing currency is that the development of the individual is his or her personal responsibility. Of course it is true that each of us has to take charge of our destiny; this is one of the big changes that has occurred over the last fifteen years. Many people in the seventies believed that their development as a practitioner of whatever calling they were following was the responsibility of the organisation to which they had committed themselves. But no organisation can achieve the continual rate of improvement and of change, the keys to competitive success, unless its people are also growing and changing. This task of coaching the individual will remain a major managerial responsibility, almost irrespective of what changes in organisational concepts apply. It is ironic that although this fact is understood, so little attention is given to the process of coaching; I know of no books or courses which help the manager to learn and apply this important skill. The process of enhancing the skills, abilities and confidence of the players in the orchestra is a combined challenge to the players, to their conductor and to the leaders of the sections.

SEVEN Rehearsals

While the British approach to management is relatively casual compared to our international competitors, it is in our attitudes to training that the most obvious differences appear. There appears to be a deeply rooted antipathy to training in the UK, both on the part of the managers and of those to be trained. It is possible that this stems from historical attitudes. We have always admired the effortless amateur who can 'beat the professional at his own game' and we have always been somewhat contemptuous of intellectuals and academics. 'Real men' in our folklore are men of action, and we admire physical courage more than moral integrity. But there is no doubt in my mind that training in Britain is a grossly undervalued source of competitive advantage.

Not only are well-trained people an asset, but an unprofessional team cannot hope to take on the best and win. We still seem to think that a 'Dad's Army' can take on the business equivalents of the SAS and the Commandos. Training is often looked upon by managers as an expensive and optional extra, and there is little basic belief that it is cost effective. Indeed, when the National Training Awards were first launched it was a real struggle to convince those who entered that they would have to demonstrate the financial effect of their training throughout their organisation. Even when you find top management who believe in training, their ideas about the time and effort which should be spent on it are wildly different from those of other countries. It is quite rare for a British business to spend more than two per cent of its payroll budget on training and development, where our competitors would think something between 10 and 20 per cent more appropriate. We have a mythical belief in on-the-job training, but even there we do not structure or organise our training efforts with any care. We think, as we do in many cases with apprenticeships, that putting a young person with someone experienced will automatically transfer knowledge and theory. We fail to realise that what happens is that the bad practices accumulated over the years get handed on and on and on.

There is no doubt that most of the development of the individual has to take place through continual coaching and careful selection of the tasks and challenges the newcomer is asked to take up. There is also no doubt that it is difficult to teach adults a new subject in an academic or intellectual sense, because the belief that once we leave university there is nothing more to learn seems to be deeply embedded. That we should continue learning after leaving school is seen as an admission that we have not taken enough advantage of the educational opportunities we had. But with the explosion of knowledge which is occurring almost all professionals need retreads of their experience. As I have said the half life of an electronic engineer is now considered about three and a half years, which means that one half of everything being taught has been superseded or enhanced by new knowledge. Of course electronic engineering is probably the fastest moving of all areas of technology. But if you look at, say, accountancy or mechanical engineering, you will find the same increasing rate of change – swift obsolescence of acquired knowledge and its replacement by new and more refined thinking.

Training appears to be viewed as something to be done to others, rather than something for oneself, and in a surprising number of areas there is ferocious resistance to the idea that a training course might be appropriate. Yet a host of specific experiences, knowledge and skills can only be transmitted by properly organised training. Our attitude to training is all too often exemplified in the selection of those we employ as training managers. Unlike the Services, where an appointment to a training establishment is seen as a stepping stone to higher rank, an appointment as a training manager in business is often seen as the end of the road. It is given as a 'quiet option' to the manager who has gone off the boil, who has suffered a heart attack or who was simply blocking the way for a younger man. Yet, just as the country derives its values and its ability to compete in the world from its teachers and its educational system, so does a business depend on the abilities, qualities and knowledge of its people. If the attitude of the management to training is so myopic, what of the attitude of those to be trained?

In Britain it appears to cause deep concern when it is suggested that an individual should go on a training course. Almost the first reaction is to assume they are being told that they are performing inadequately the task they have been given. Far from training being seen as an investment in the individual, it is often seen as an adverse comment on performance. The peer pressure against self-improvement, particularly on the shop floor, is intense, and the individual will often have to cope with comments such as 'What's the matter with us then?', 'Why are we not good enough for you?', 'Why do you want to improve yourself?', 'Do you want to be a boss's boy?'. But perhaps the biggest switch-off is the lack of confidence in our abilities to assimilate new skills. One of the unfortunate legacies of our educational system is that the vast majority of us leave school more aware of what we cannot do than what we can. Far from creating a national reserve of winners, who have the self-confidence to believe they can master any subject or task, we seem to impress in people's minds a conviction of their limitations rather than a belief in their potential. This is not just an attitude which one sees on the shop floor; all too often managers who are offered training courses either refuse or go reluctantly and with deep cynicism, because they fear being exposed in front of their peers. They would rather attack the entire concept of training or, more damagingly, the course they are attending, than risk exposure. I have been amazed to see some of the most intelligent people totally opposed to joining others on a course which is well within their intellectual grasp. I have known people whose

118

only question on being offered training is 'Will there be a test?'. The fear of failing an examination is engendered in most people from the earliest age. Examinations are seen as tests to demonstrate our inadequacy rather than for any other purpose, and competitive marking is one of the biggest single turn-offs.

We therefore have a background, from both the managers and those to be trained, which could hardly be less propitious for the acquisition of skills and knowledge on which future competitiveness between companies will be based. Just as in an orchestra a single unskilled player can spoil the effect, so with business. Any business is only as strong as its weakest link, and that weak link can exist anywhere in the organisation – be it the despatch clerk, the telephone operator, the process worker, or the managing director. Not only do we have to be fully competitive as a team, but each member of that team has to be at least as good as their opposite number in the competing team. And even if each individual is skilled in his or her own particular field, the competitiveness of the whole will depend upon the ability of the man at the top to turn this range of skills into a cohesive team. But without updating of basic skills there is no chance of creating a winning team. There is no possibility, no matter how good their conductor, that a bunch of people who have not yet learnt to play their instruments properly are going to produce a world-beating orchestral rendition. This comes only after they have mastered their particular instruments and have been extensively coached

119

and rehearsed to produce a successful contribution to the whole.

The fears outlined are widespread in this country (more so than in many other places where I have operated), which makes both the necessity for training and the training itself more difficult. The job of the teacher is not only to impart knowledge – that is a relatively small part of the total. The main task is to stimulate the interest and gain the commitment and involvement of the pupil. If the business pupil approaches the acquisition of new knowledge in a negative frame of mind, determined to reject rather than to involve themselves, the trainer's job is almost impossible.

Your first approaches to training your people will therefore have to break this mental log-jam, which we in Britain have brought upon ourselves. So much money spent on training has been wasted. Sitting down a bunch of tired, uninterested and uninvolved individuals in a room at the end of a long day's work, and then reading a series of exhortations and showing a series of diagrams is unlikely to produce cost-effective results. Training should be about engaging the minds of individuals and involving them in the acquisition of skills they need not only to make a success of their job but a success of their lives. There is a curious lack of aspiration amongst people, a belief that so many things are beyond them and that attempting to overcome the disadvantages they have been born to is a waste of time. We have to break this cycle if our training is to be effective, and we

120

have to make our training more effective if our businesses' are going to be able to compete against the best in the world.

Under these circumstances there is a chronic temptation to opt out all together. Since the role of the manager as coach is well established, and most managers who have learnt how to grow people take pleasure and satisfaction from their achievements, there is an understandable fear of involving others in the development process. There is also the perennial problem that people will be taught to expect attitudes and ways of doing things which, on their return to work, they will find are not followed in their place of work. They will therefore become disillusioned, or dissatisfied with tasks with which they were previously happy. This dissatisfaction is an essential ingredient of change, but the danger arises if it continues and attempts to apply new found skills meet with no interest or success. Not only have you wasted the money spent on the training, but you are worse off than when you started. At the least, the employee will have become even more cynical about the chances of changing things, and at the extreme he will leave to find somewhere where his skills can more easily be applied. I believe that training should be aimed at the individual and, although there are examples of organisations which achieve good results from standard arrangements for large groups of people, on balance one has to find a way in which the individual will buy in to the training provided.

As if the foregoing problems were not enough there is also the perennial concern of managers that as soon as an employee is more fully qualified and trained he or she will

121

use their enhanced market value to move elsewhere for better pay. This is an understandable concern, but the remedy cannot lie in keeping people operating below their capabilities. If your organisation cannot provide the challenges and opportunities, people will vote with their feet in any event. The solution lies in the way in which you organise reward and motivate your people. It is inevitable that an able person will often be approached by head-hunters and others in an attempt to lure them away, but good men and women are quick to realise the advantages of continuing with a business which has broadened their horizons and opportunities. In this respect a reputation for growing your people is more likely to keep them than a misguided attempt to hold them beneath their capabilities. People leave because they feel they are not getting anywhere. The argument is thus much stronger for making the training relevant to needs and future tasks, for that is the best way of ensuring a return on your investment and efforts.

My own preferred solution to this is that every person in an organisation, from top to bottom, should have an annual training profile. This is probably best made at the time of the annual 'counselling chat'. After discussing the successes (and possible failures) for the year, it is a good idea to turn the discussion to what other skills would have been helpful. The manager will have his own ideas as to what might be good things for the employee to learn or study, but in a surprising number of cases the individual will confess that he or she wishes to learn more about something quite different. I am constantly surprised by the varieties of subjects

122

people wish to understand better. Hardly anybody below senior or financial management understands how to read a balance sheet and set of company accounts. Even the costing systems in your own organisation are frequently not understood, but absolutely everyone knows how to work the job number and what items will slide through without creating a fuss. Similarly people will often admit that they are uncomfortable speaking in front of an audience, are unhappy about their ability to write a report or a letter, conduct an interview or meet new faces. A course which meets an individual's professed interests and requirements is three-quarters of the way there. He arrives wanting to learn, his attention fully engaged, and does not look on the training as a waste of time. Moreover, a training profile which leads to action enhances the individual's sense of self-worth and the reputation of the organisation for listening, caring and taking action. It really is a win-win situation.

Even when the manager has strong views about what should be the first additional skill to be learnt, it is wise to try to plant the notion tactfully so that the individual feels that the idea has come from him, rather than being a direct request from his boss. Many training courses of a day or two days are more than adequate to begin the process of learning. Nor should the advantages of modern technology be forgotten. It is now possible to learn from computers and other systems (such as the Open University) which do not need the physical presence of a teacher. There are two real advantages to these methods of learning. Firstly, the instructor can be the best in the field and a real expert in the ways in which complicated ideas can be assimilated by the student. Secondly, and perhaps even more importantly, the student can learn at a comfortable pace, a point can be covered repeatedly without embarrassment or holding up others, and the learner can move on to the next issue only when they are thoroughly convinced that they understand the preceding facts. Anyone who has learnt a language through Linguaphone tapes is familiar with the concept, but the availability of computers, CDs and television has increased the power of this method of training immeasurably. Many years ago I was amazed at the initiative of a works manager of mine who made distance learning facilities available for his people on a whole variety of basic educational subjects – chemistry, mathematics, English and so on. I confessed to being cynical that the mere provision of the facilities would produce the response he expected. How wrong I was! In no time at all every course was oversubscribed and he had to make more facilities available. He had tapped hunger for self-improvement, and remember that these were not subjects directly related to success at work, nor was financial inducement of any sort offered to the individual who sought to improve his or her basic educational skills. The point was exactly that. Individuals were not being required to study, nor did they feel that they were going to be judged on their performance, and they therefore felt comfortable with the learning process. Another large organisation I knew decided that their people needed better language skills. They made what proved to be a rash promise that anybody who wished to learn a language would be helped to do so by the company.

They had expected a response of under one hundred, but nearly three quarters of the company lined up to take advantage of the proposal. To their credit they honoured their commitment, and this must be one of the very few organisations in this country which is truly multilingual, even though many of the languages were chosen because of holiday interests or other non-work-related concerns. The point of course was that, having learnt one language, their fear of learning had been removed and they speedily went on to absorb others.

Although, for the reasons I have outlined, I believe that training is best done on an individual basis, I have encountered some remarkable examples of companies where an overall training profile for an experienced member of the organisation has been sold in a very sophisticated manner. I recently visited a joint American and Japanese company operating in this country. The workforce were all solid Northerners, but they seemed to combine the best working and operating habits of both their owners. It was of course a single status factory, where everybody wore the same working rig, but I noticed that on their jacket breast pocket each wore a sort of pie-chart, with varying sectors filled in. The sectors of the pie-chart represented training courses which were available to any employee, and the fully trained individual – be he a manager or a member of the shop floor – had filled in the entire circle. Not only was this a mark of distinction, but it meant that the training profile of any individual in any section was on permanent display in the place of work. If it became necessary to provide cover for somebody who was absent a quick check indicated who had done the training necessary to take the job over. I was intrigued with the concept and asked whether any reward was offered for the completion of the different courses. The question was greeted with Bateman cartoon-like disbelief. Of course not. So what incentive was there to the individual to undertake a course? The answer was, witheringly, that all their people wanted to become better at their jobs and they recognised the relevance of the courses to being able to do a broader range of tasks. The esteem of their peers was gained by being a fully operational allrounder, whom everybody knew could be relied upon to do any job. There peer pressure fell on the individual who lacked the get-up-and-go to acquire a full portfolio of skills. It has to be acknowledged that the skills that I am talking about in this factory were mainly operating ones, although some sectors of the pie chart did involve other areas of expertise.

The Japanese approach to basic training is very different from ours. Nobody is allowed near an assembly line, or allowed to start on any production job, until he has practised exhaustively in a training centre and everybody is confident that he has the full range of manual and other skills necessary to slot in without causing any disruption. An assembly line job in a Japanese factory is viewed as a highly skilled task which requires commensurate levels of training. If you join an average British company you will be given brief instruction in how to use a nut winder, shown where the bin of

126

bolts are and told the number of bolts that you have to apply at your particular work station.

Contrast this with the induction process in a Japanese car line. You start in a mock-up training centre where you are taught, painfully and methodically, to pick up an exact number of nuts in one grab, without looking at the nut bin. In one case I know of you are expected to pick up exactly nine nuts at a time and you do not progress to the next stage until you can do that in your sleep, so to speak. You are then taught to hold the nine nuts with one hand while winding them on with a nut winder held in the other. Only when you can complete the entire operation, which may well take a week of continual and repetitive practice, are you allowed near the assembly line. This level of training is for a job which is generally rated to be one of the simplest ones, and the amounts of training which are required for difficult jobs takes even longer. I have asked how much in advance a factory would start preparing for the introduction of a new model and was told that training would start about a year before the model was due to be launched. While of course there is continual pressure to improve the production rate once the model is produced, nevertheless, not a single model will be made in earnest until the whole workforce have practised endlessly their contributions to the process.

This attention to manual dexterity and the ability to do the job right each time, coupled with dedication to speed and effectiveness is not, however, the end of their approach to training. Since factories of this type depend on Kaizen, steady improvement of the process and product in every

127

way, they expect their people to understand far more than the manual problems of winding on nine nuts in different positions on an assembly line moving at x feet per minute. The ultimate objective is to have every worker skilled in every activity, so that he or she can understand the inter-relationship between the actions necessary to produce the finished product. They are also required to know and understand the testing procedures, the way the products are designed, the costing systems, and where the major elements of cost are in the process. The acquisition of this broad span of knowledge is not just a bit of paternalistic 'nice to know' stuff; it is the fundamental basis by which improvements are carried out. Improvement in the best internationally competitive factories is not something driven purely from the top; it is the aim of every single member of the staff and workforce to find ways to change and improve current practice. It is a far cry indeed from the under-used 'Suggestion Scheme', where workers put in suggestions, usually regarding safety or housekeeping, and are rewarded with an encouragement bonus. In many Japanese factories the changes suggested are of the most fundamental type, sometimes involving total re-design by other departments, and it is because each individual is in a position to view the totality of the operation that he or she feels free to make such broad-ranging contributions. It cannot be emphasised enough that competition for the future is not going to be in the manual dexterity of different groups of people. It will mean the involvement of the creativity, experience,

128

understanding and commitment of every man and woman in the organisation.

In a go-ahead organisation training should not be limited to the activities in-house. A visit or secondment by some of your operators to work on a customer's line, or on a supplier's line, produces almost unbelievable benefits in terms of improved relationships and understanding. The companies that will succeed in the future are those which understand the interdependence of all the people in the supply chain, from the final customer right back to the raw material suppliers. It is the ability to operate this chain as one, albeit in a flexible way, that will give the true advantages in speed of response, predictability of quality, immediacy of delivery, and so on. Many of these sources of competitive advantage are attitudes of mind, but attitudes of mind do not appear as if by magic, they have to be instilled, repeated, shown by example and trained for constantly and consistently. We need much broader concepts of the training process, and the contribution it can make to our ability to win the competitive battle.

Managers need training in training. They need training in developing their people and they need to understand a great deal more about the processes by which people learn, and how they become committed and involved in the process of learning. Even though in the past we have all recognised that some managers are outstandingly good at developing their people, in the future that will be a source of real reward rather than merely a bonus point. Indeed those who are good at developing their subordinates are frequently rewarded by

129

being left in the same hierarchical position so that the company does not lose the advantages of the in-house training school. There is no reason why such a formidable contribution should not be recognised and rewarded in the same way that other more directly tangible contributions are seen as grounds for promotion or special reward.

Just as with everything else in business, it is important to get more out of training than achievement of the single objective of improving one area of skill. Properly thought out and managed, training involves a great deal more, and can be a major influence on the building of the team. Training is something which can be done by every level of an organisation simultaneously. The need to learn to present one's ideas in public applies to every department, every skill and every level of a company. It is possible, therefore, to have a public speaking course of, say, six people which could involve shop stewards, a foreman, an accountant, a research scientist and so on. The experience of learning something together creates a mutuality of understanding which far exceeds anything to be gained from the normal interaction of work. Some of the problems of creating teams arise from the compartmentalisation of the ways most people operate. They have a network of people with whom they co-operate continuously and whom they think they know well, but each is dependent upon the activities of large numbers of other people, who are almost automatically assumed to be less capable than those within your own network. Nothing breaks down barriers more than the realisation that we all have the ability to learn a new skill at roughly the same speed, and that each of us has something to contribute to the whole.

In other books I have given the example of a game played on one of the training courses I attended, which involved the building of a tower with Lego bricks. On our team we happened to have a highly qualified structural engineer, who approached the problem from a theoretical point of view and was quickly defeated by a foreman, who had a son who was a Lego brick enthusiast. The juxtaposition between practical and theoretical experience is something which is of value to every aspect of business, and the best solutions are ones which incorporate the contribution of each approach. So training courses should not be looked upon as just meeting the needs of an individual, they should contribute to the achievement of the objectives of the whole business.

The role of training and team-building is not confined to enabling individuals in different sections of work to meet one another on 'neutral ground'. Properly thought-out training courses and systems give a common language and help to impart a sense of common values, as well as the mutuality of respect which is the basis all teamwork. These aims are achieved only by giving considerable thought to the training process. Perhaps the primary role of the manager or the training manager in a large organisation is to be constantly scanning the horizon to find out what is available and to pick the training courses, methods and locations which will best suit the values and ambience of his company. I know numbers of companies who feel that their people have benefited by the wholesale use of courses provided by the

Leadership Trust. The selection of courses and training methods is a key decision and warrants the same thought and involvement by top managers as any other key decision in the business. At an earlier stage of my career, when I needed to create more cohesiveness among a large number of people responding to disparate organisations, I attended every course I could find which I thought might help to achieve my objectives. The time was not wasted. Even the courses I rejected taught me something, and indeed I believe it is difficult to find any training experience from which one does not gain some immediate advantage. These advantages come from training interposed with practical experience – a sort of two-way stretch of benefit both to the trainers and to those being trained. The trainers have a steady feedback about the practical difficulties and applications of what they are teaching, while the trainees appreciate more clearly the impact of the theoretical ideas, or the new concepts they are being taught, on their place of work.

It is for this reason that I greatly favour sandwich courses, or MBA courses, for mature students who have had some practical experience. If you decide that the MBA route is a useful one for your company, it is as well to build a relationship with a training organisation or school who will take the trouble to understand your particular needs. In extreme cases many business schools will lay on specifically tailored courses. But in many cases some of the advantages of an external training organisation of this type are gained by your people meeting and interacting with people from other companies and other countries. I made extensive use of INSEAD at Fontainbleu as a means of exposing British managers to their European counterparts and The International Management Institute at Geneva for people who would have to operate in the less developed parts of the world and needed a greater understanding, for example, of the conditions pertaining in South America, Africa or parts of Asia.

The question of extended courses is controversial. In almost any organisation there are some people who will benefit from attending a business school, but if they are to do so it may be a good idea to try to meet more than one training objective at a time. A school which has a breadth of international appeal or specific cultural and geographical experience may well fill in another gap in a trainee's background at the same time. However one looks at training it is an expensive investment, both for the company and for the individual; it warrants at least as much care and attention as would be applied to the purchase of a new machine tool, or to capital investment. For that is what training is; investment in the capital of the knowledge and skills of your people, your company's recipe for competitive success.

EIGHT Playing in Harmony

Every company faces the problem of reconciling the interests and perceptions of the individual with the needs of the group they work in and the overall requirements of the business. The greater the congruence between these different points of view, the greater the effectiveness of the company as a whole, and this increase is almost on a geometric scale. A small increase in harmony will give a large boost to effectiveness. We have all had the sad and salutary experience of working in outfits which are at sixes and sevens and have been aware of how little of our potential we were able to contribute. But teamwork is not easy, partly because of the different expectations and perceptions of individuals. What has the most direct meaning for most people is the clarity of the goal and the ability of the individual to 'buy in' to it. Given that, one's own approach to work is heavily influenced by the chemistry of the team one is working in, the organisation and the freedom for individual initiative and the recognition accorded to good or bad work. Each individual will see these factors from a different angle and it is not possible or desirable to tune a system so that everyone's view is the same. The needs of the team are affected by the mix of temperaments and the balance of the team and, of course, by the skills, caprices and whims of the team leader. The requirements of the business are in theory met by the selection of the people and their organisational structure. The difficulty is that business needs vary and change at an ever increasing rate, while organisational structure changes only slowly. Creating harmony from all of these elements is akin to juggling with three balls. The juggler succeeds only when all three balls are in play at once.

Plainly, every company has to have a large number of 'trade offs' between the effect on the individual, the needs of the group and the requirements of the business. These 'trade offs' cannot be limitless, even if the mathematical combinations of individuals, organisation and reward appear infinite. Some principles have to prevail even if (as I tend to favour) one is prepared to accept a degree of chaos in the interests of speed and flexibility. Almost every person in an organisation, including the management, yearns for clarity. There is a general hope that somewhere there is an all-seeing, all-powerful individual who is directing the myriad worker ants to create a beautiful harmony from their individual and apparently disparate efforts. This is often expressed in terms of 'You just tell me what you want me to do and I'll do it', or 'Why don't they make their minds up'. Such yearning for order and clarity is understandable, but it contrasts with our wish for 'freedom' and the ability to exercise our choices and affect the group we are working with.

There is total polarisation between a rigidly hierarchical, closely defined and heavily controlled set-up, and the loose, well-trained, adjustable and flexible organisation, which is what people tend to gravitate towards. To return to my analogy of the orchestra. The orchestra really begins to work when each individual feels that he or she is contributing to their full artistic capacity and yet collaborating with their colleagues to produce something more beautiful than could be produced individually. Anybody who has sung in a choir or played in a musical group knows the effect that the players, the conductor and the score have on one another. We desperately need to achieve this effect in our business world, and for it to be strong enough to endure through an endless series of new pieces played in different tempos and different moods – and sometimes not even finished. Sadly, when we sit down in business to play a symphony the audience (our customers) often indicate that they want a different piece before we manage to finish the first movement. Woe betide us if we continue playing the original piece, or if we assume that the reason for the customer's choice was dissatisfaction with our playing. We have to understand why the piece of music needs changing, but the style and the empathy must be maintained.

Each of these aspects of business is a subject in its own right. Let us start by looking at the problems involved in getting the chemistry of the team right. Without question the ability to work in teams and to swiftly adapt and change them will be one of the keys to commercial success for the future. It is essential that the company ethos and value system encourage these abilities. To some degree the problem of working in a team is self resolving, because most people will not continue to work in a group where they do not feel a degree of empathy. Business values are the absolute key to teams working effectively. I was struck by this fact in my early days in ICI when I was selected to work with representatives of the other divisions in a series of business exhibitions being undertaken in the former USSR. Even though we all came from different parts of the company, with different individual histories, and from businesses with different characteristics, because of our shared commitment to the ideals of our company we found it remarkably easy to settle down and work together as a group of peers.

Prima donnas do not fit into teams and, if they are necessary for furtherance of the business, their positioning in relationship to other people requires considerable thought and care. Apart from the company values, which are the backdrop to the whole of personnel management, a vital decision is made when a new appointment is made to an existing group. The considerations which must be borne in mind when making such an appointment are, as always, wide and varied. The composition of the group is always looked at in terms of its skill base and the appointment may be made to replace an individual who has been playing a particular role and brought a particular background of experience and skills to bear. When appointing new people it is essential to recognise that, while no appointment should be for ever, one which lasts less than three years should really be considered a failure. Every time a new person is appointed to a team, the nature of the team suffers such a degree of change that it is important to have some idea of what the change may be and to ensure that it will be helpful to the business aims, rather than harmful.

Since the whole of business is about change, no appointment should ever seem to be a straight replacement for the man who has gone before. It is an opportunity to create a new input and to make a shift in how the team works, as well as in a larger business sense. Appointments therefore call for considerable understanding of the way the group is working at the present time, as well as business clarity about the changes necessary for continued success a few years ahead. Those making the appointments therefore need to canvass views on these factors from more than one person, even though the manager of the outfit will always have the ultimate say on the person who is appointed. But, although the chemistry with the manager is important, it cannot and must not be the only consideration, otherwise even the best of companies speedily descend into 'cronyism', with all that it involves.

Business life is never comfortable, indeed it is time to start worrying when everything seems cosy. Some degree of friction and conflict is vital for progress, but too much friction can be as harmful as none. One has to aim for a middle point if the organisation is to move ahead. The greater the degree of mutual respect and trust, the higher the level of friction an organisation can tolerate. The right level of friction is the critical component for the maintenance of speed and change, but it is a sensitive adjustment – a trifle too much can quickly have a disproportionate negative effect. Very few managers willingly seek to add somebody to their team whom they recognise will be an irritant. Nevertheless, this is one of the ingredients which often need to be introduced, at an appropriate and tolerable level. We have all seen teams of people who have worked together, initially with success, who become more and more comfortable with each other and the way they do things. Merely replacing one individual is enough to destroy this cosiness. Initially things will be changed as a result of the friction caused by the newcomer and his irritating habit of questioning long established perceived wisdom. Looking back on my career, I can think of many cases where I was used by my superiors in this sort of way, but perhaps the best examples come from the *Troubleshooter* TV series. In every case imparting my views on the need for change involved friction. It says a great deal for my friends from Copella and the Churchill Pottery Company that their dedication to their business and their people was sufficient for them to take and act on unpalatable advice. They had more or less asked me to join their team in the knowledge that advice would be given which they might not like and I respect them for it.

This is one of the reasons why managers should be encouraged to have a considerable amount of consultation, both at their peer level and with their superiors, before appointments are made. More often than not the frictions that prove harmful to the progress of an organisation derive from faults in personal chemistry. As though this were not in itself complex enough, a further consideration has to be the effect on the individual, as a person and on his career development. Creating teams is a bit like cookery. The dish being concocted needs a mix of ingredients, but the art in putting the dish together will be the subtle variants in the quantity and quality of the ingredients and in the manner in which they are combined. Like everything else in business, appointing and setting up a team is an art rather than a science. There will always be a wish, both from the point of view of the team and of the boss, to optimise the team in one particular direction, but it is the mixture which matters rather than a theoretical optimisation of one facet.

The mind of the manager will be primarily on the need to fill the gap in technical input from which his team is suffering. 'Old so-and-so was absolutely first class, but he was not really up to the current trends in information technology,' or whatever it may be. The team may have a more urgent need in the area of balance between optimism and pessimism, listening or dynamic intervention, impatience and broad-brush view versus concern about getting the detail right, humour versus seriousness, sensitivity within the company and to customers and suppliers, as opposed to brash determination to push on regardless. All these characteristics are necessary in a balanced team and it is seldom that one is able to play three-dimensional chess and meet every requirement. Ideally, of course, the person you require will be right up to date on current developments in information technology, have a good working knowledge of Spanish, a good track record of working with and the respect of customer X, be known and respected by supplier Y, introduce

141

a welcome leavening of humour into your team and get on well with each individual. Listed like this, it is small wonder that our appointments seldom add up to everything that we had hoped for; it is on the ability to find an individual with a balance of these factors that team building at the appointment level depends.

But it also depends on something else. Before making the appointment, the individuals concerned should spend time thinking what it will do for the person appointed. Of course we cannot ensure that every move made and every task an individual is required to perform will necessarily be to the immediate advantage of his or her personal development. Nevertheless the corollary is equally untrue. Unless the job, the team and the chemistry all contain the opportunity for personal growth it is unlikely that the individual concerned will perform well in the job you are seeking to create. This question of the development of the individual can be helped enormously if you know something of the dynamics of team building. The problem is that all too often your expectation of the new man will be that he will replace old Bloggs and, as such, the sooner he 'settles in', adjusts to the way the team works and thinks and proves a carbon copy of Bloggs and Bloggs's winning ways, the more pleased everybody will be. Of course it never works like that. The new individual will have quite different characteristics from those you came to know and love in 'Bloggs'. In fact, if he is to be worth his salt he has to have a different effect on the team. The onus lies at least as much on the team to adapt to him as it does on him to adapt. The reality of a member joining a

142

new team is that the team will have to adjust a bit and the new individual will have to adjust a lot. Unless this happens, you will fail to keep the dynamic of improvement in your group and you will also fail to satisfy the new joiner.

Approaching team building in this way places a great stress on the manager and great responsibility to orchestrate the work of the team and coach the new individual so that the appropriate balance is found. It is unlikely that this will happen unless the manager understands the processes at work and that the new arrival must indeed be a catalyst to keep the team moving ahead. After all, at minimum, if the newcomer has just been promoted, he has the most recent direct experience of how things look from below and the worries and concerns of that level. This is knowledge which has a very short half-life, so everybody else would be well advised to listen to the individual on what the current views are about their performance, procedures and relevance to the business. It is frequently an unwelcome shock, and the skill with which these messages are passed on will reflect on both the team leader and the appointee.

Of course teams are not necessarily related to each other in a direct hierarchical manner. I have talked here primarily of the new appointment to a job where there is a clear boss, but a great deal of work in a modern business environment is done between networks and peer groups of equals, choosing to collaborate to be more effective. Here it is much more difficult to design the team in the way that is helpful when a new appointment is made. For better or worse you have to use the guys who are already in position, who happen to have the relevant experience and the relevant personalities to further the task for which the network is being set up. The skills and perceptions required for working in this way are similar to those required in an entirely new company, with the difference that in a network of peers there is seldom clear managerial responsibility. However, you will speedily discern a real leader who has established himself or herself as the prime mover by their effectiveness and adaptability. Team working is a considerable art; it involves the individual in learning the necessary skills, and team leaders in understanding how to foster teamwork. I have often believed that although courses in leadership are necessary, courses in 'followership' would be a useful part of the business environment. There is skill involved in being a team member, just as there are levels of skills in being a team leader. Team members need coaching, advice, help and process understanding if they are to realise their full potential.

There will, however, always be the odd solo flyer who cannot work in a team at all. It is hopeless trying to build teams of people with incompatible personal characteristics or deep personal enmities, or indeed to create a team from solo flyers. If a man is incapable of working with others, you must consider very seriously whether it is sensible to employ him in any role. Unless you are sure that there are roles which can be filled by the solitary individual, you are better to take a rain-check and encourage the individual to look elsewhere. In my experience there are very few people who are total loners; if they are, it is usually because of

144

their single minded involvement with their own ideas and technology. It may be perfectly possible to employ such an individual as a specialist available for consultation but not expected to involve himself with others in an ongoing collaborative way. However, in modern companies there are fewer and fewer reasons to carry such specialist contributors within the organisation. These skills are more frequently bought in from consultants or specialists, rather than carrying such a person in-house.

As I pointed out earlier, one of the problems with organisation is that it has to be a function of the current business objectives. Formal organisational change requires huge disruption and upheaval, which most individuals find extremely difficult to deal with. It is for this reason that this sort of change occurs so seldom. Nevertheless, the theoretical structure of a company and the way it works are barely recognisable as the same thing. It is all these pressures which have forced companies to look more and more to 'non-organisations' of various sorts. Above everything organisations have to be flexible and able to accommodate vast changes of business objectives. Moreover, they must encourage ease of working between the various segments of the business, all of whom have to collaborate successfully if the business is to succeed against its top competitors.

The decline of the long hierarchy has been forced by three major business considerations. The first and prime mover has been the realisation of the high costs of carrying large numbers of people supervising the work of others. The hierarchy derived from military organisations and was then intensified by business theories such as the limits of 'span of control' (the number of people who could report directly to a single individual). Although the pressures to reduce hierarchical levels derive from cost, I believe that cost is the least important reason for reducing hierarchy. I have long been an advocate of flat non-hierarchical organisations, and my obsession with such organisational concepts stems from two different considerations. The first, and perhaps the most important, is the question of speed. Long chains of command simply cannot react quickly. No matter how you draw the theoretical reasons for having a long chain of command the reality is that the decisions are taken further and further away from the points of maximum knowledge of the detail required. A flat non-hierarchical organisation need not involve people who have nothing to add to the decision and will inevitably hold up the decision-making process while they inform, reassure and accustom themselves to a level of risk with which they may feel uncomfortable. Speed is now recognised everywhere as a major source of competitive advantage and speed of reaction, of response and of change are aided immeasurably by having fewer and fewer numbers of people involved in the decision-making. Speed also results from lack of rigidity in organisational terms and from the ability to decide which matters really do need to go to the top for decision.

This book is not about business organisation; it is about managing people and the factors which affect them. Nothing affects the individual more than his perception of the degree of organisational space he has to operate in. This, coupled with speed, is the main reason for favouring the flat non-hierarchical organisation. It is also the thinking behind 'buzz words' such as empowerment. There is no doubt that individuals respond best to a situation where they feel that they have power as well as responsibility. The trap into which businesses repeatedly fall is to pass responsibility down the line without giving people the power to carry out that responsibility. This is one of the greatest sources of disillusionment with concepts of empowerment. Nothing is more dispiriting, or acts as a greater disincentive, than to be given a responsibility you relish, or even one you believe slightly beyond your capabilities, and then to find that what you need to do to carry out that responsibility has to be referred to someone who has command over the actions you wish to take.

The good modern organisation does not have job descriptions, but job responsibilities. A considerable amount of 'fuzz' is left around the organisation so that the freedom of action of the individual is not constrained. Of course no organisation can afford to pass full responsibility for everything down the line to people who may be learning on the job. That is where the coach comes in – the middle manager who keeps an eye on what is happening and blows the whistle before disaster strikes. Nevertheless, if a man or woman is given a job to do, he or she will give of their best only if they feel that they have the necessary space around them. As I pointed out in an earlier book, space in this area is seldom taken for granted. Most people have been taught to think more readily about what the individual cannot do,

147

what 'they' would not accept, and the limitations on their power, rather than on their freedom to deliver the goods.

The most effective organisational structure, which will enable the speed and adaptability on which business success depends, is one where the ownership of the responsibility has been transferred as far down the line as is conceivably possible. In many cases this involves passing responsibilities hitherto considered to be managerial ones down to people on the shop floor. Experience in organisations which have done this shows that an increased level of responsibility creates a greater sense of commitment to the success of the company than attempts to compartmentalise and then to co-ordinate responsibilities. People right down the line have to become accustomed to thinking about the broader consider-ations of business when they are looking at how they execute their responsibilities. The only people who can co-ordinate activities are the people who carry the responsibility.

The difficulty is that there was a fad in the 1970s for forms of 'matrix' management which meant that nobody was ultimately responsible for anything. This was yet another effort to resolve the age-old problems of organis-ational precedence and clarity. Under the matrix system a manager was allegedly equally responsible to, say, the national manager for performance, and the product manager for the performance of a particular product. The two were often at variance. The national manager might want added volume to knock out a competitor in his territory, while the product manager wanted less volume and more margin. Such dichotomy was not reconcilable by the unhappy individual

148

responding to both. Attempts to resolve these issues by making the territory or the product have superior organisational power often meant that no compromise was sought and one extreme approach prevailed. I believe these attempts to prescribe solutions in organisational form seldom achieve what is needed. Both managers can be given joint responsibility for the outcome and are thus forced to take each other's needs into consideration – producing a solution which may not be perfect for either but which both can live with. Responsibilities can be assigned with considerable clarity, and the same responsibility can be assigned to more than one person. The Japanese overcome these problems because of their cultural background, which places high values on the abilities of groups to work together. Their protracted methods of decision-taking are a reflection of their wish to involve everybody, so that when the decision to move ahead is ultimately taken the ownership of each part of the problem has been accepted by those who have to carry it out. Culturally, it is unlikely that we will find it easy to adapt to this particular approach. Not only does our own inheritance lead us to value individuality rather than the ability to work within a group, but speed of change means that the individual has to take more and more responsibility for his or her own future rather than relying on others.

The whole idea of empowerment means easing back on organisational and hierarchical controls but being tougher on failure to discharge given responsibilities. This is not a comfortable way of organising or working. The individual

149

lacks the alibis that long hierarchical organisations provide. He or she is responsible for the success or failure of a part of the business, and the only definition of that responsibility is the end result. These methods of working provide headroom for the achievers but remove hiding places for those not capable of existing within the uncertainties of today's world of business. All these pressures result from the necessity to maintain speed of change and the inability of anyone to forecast the future with any accuracy; indeed, the only certainty is that the rate of change will increase. The organisational risk is much less if responsibility for sensing these changes and adapting to them is spread more widely, rather than concentrated on one alleged genius at the top, who is responsible for deciding everything, from the small tactical actions to the broad strategic thrust of where the business should be going. Masloe produced the concept of a hierarchy of needs for the individual. According to his research, the lowest part of the hierarchy – the need for some degree of personal and financial security – had to be met before the individual was motivated by less measurable but equally important needs for self realisation and so on. In the same way an organisation has a hierarchy of needs, the most important of which have to be met before the others can be achieved. In this hierarchy the organisation requires those at the top to have vision and clarity about the strategy, the ability to maintain business balance financially, and the ability to retain, select and motivate people. Down the line every individual has to fulfil his or her role within this overall framework. They have to do this with help and guidance, but not in response to an endless stream of detailed instructions.

Once a team of people is accustomed to working in this way the speed and effectiveness with which they work will increase greatly. The majority of people enjoy the scope for carrying out responsibilities and derive satisfaction from the achievement of the sub-goals which they know to be their justification for employment. However, enjoying the freedom and demands put upon one requires experience and growth within one's capabilities and expectations. The feeling of space, responsibility, ownership of the problem, trust and overall clarity about what is expected in terms of achievement, rather than conformity, has to be the aim of business organisation. There is no manual which will produce the answer; the organisation will have to flex itself continually to meet the new challenges forced upon it. The ability of a decentralised, empowered group of people to adapt and achieve this flexibility is of a different order from that of the closely controlled, hierarchically dominated, organisation, and ultimately will grow the people and the response needed.

NINE The Applause

As so often in life, the aspect of managing people which attracts the most attention, the most debate and the most theories – namely pay and rewards – is also the one which seldom achieves the ambitions that are held for it. There are a host of complex reasons why this may be so. The first one is, of course, that pay and conditions are set in a competitive marketplace where not only does the individual relate his pay to that of his peers in other departments of the same company, but also people in the same company are constantly comparing their pay and conditions with those they believe to be obtainable elsewhere. Just to make life more complicated all these factors are continuously moving. Many companies have got into the habit of having a single pay adjustment once a year for everyone – usually timed, of all the infelicitous ideas, at Christmas. This timing further compounds the complexities of an already intricate problem of relative dynamic movement. Christmas is, after all, the season of goodwill and people are even less likely at Christmas than at any other time of the year to take kindly to giving or receiving bad news.

153

However, these are not the primary reasons for the apparent failures of our payment systems. Because payment systems so seldom satisfy, and even less frequently motivate, there is a great urge on the part of pay administrators to seek predictable parity in allocating and setting pay. Countless bureaucratic methods have been used to seek this philosopher's stone, usually with extremely complex mathematical calculations which will enable the exact relative worth of every individual to be placed in a provable context. The contract has to be acceptable to the individual, and yet limit the perennial onward march of one of the most important cost elements of the whole business: the wages and salaries bill. It is this urge for demonstrable fairness which seems to me to add enormously to the overall difficulties. The irony is that within practically every group of people the three best performers and the three worst could unhesitatingly be nominated by almost every member of the group. The variance of opinion in that area would be extremely small and yet, if you asked people to grade every individual in a group in the exact order of their contribution or effectiveness, there is no chance whatsoever that you would get any broad consensus of agreement. However, a system in which everybody is payed the same except the top three and the bottom three does not satisfy the urge to try and mark small elements of difference and is considered arbitrary and unfair. The problem is exacerbated by the fact that everyone's assessments are usually carried out at the same time and are meant to cover a full year's work. However assiduous the attempt, to take into account absolutely everything that an individual has contributed over a whole year is extraordinarily difficult. The experiences of the last few weeks or months are uppermost in one's mind and there is a natural tendency to apply a greater emphasis to those recent events than to an occasion earlier in the year when something particularly good was done.

The appraisal itself is hard enough without the additional pressures upon the assessor. After all, in the case of an assessment for a pay award, the individual concerned will, at minimum, be informed of the overall outcome of your judgement, and at maximum they will see a written report on which this outcome will be based. One of the characteristics of British people is a great dislike of causing affront to others. Hardly anybody in the United Kingdom likes to be the purveyor of the bad news. Bosses shoot them, and subordinates hate them. Very few British people see the blunt statement of an individual's opinions as a compliment to the recipient and a valuable opportunity to be able to contest the view that has been expressed. We are happier by far trying to 'soften the blow' by obfuscating the clarity of our remarks. We do this despite the abundant evidence that people do not easily or readily digest bad news. Most of us have a God-given switch-off mechanism which enables us to misunderstand criticism totally. We cling on to the kindly words which are meant to soften the blow with such grim determination that we miss the blow altogether. The realities of this sort of behaviour, which I feel confident will be recognised by every reader, are that we miss the opportunity to understand what is being said and hence to rectify whatever it is that is causing our problems.

In my view, fair treatment of an individual means that he or she has every right to know, as closely as you can convey, what are the things he or she can do better, and what is the best course to take for the man or woman concerned in order to further their own interests. No business ever prospered by holding back the individuals who go to make up the business. Businesses can prosper only when every man and woman in the business is growing and developing, and is therefore giving of his or her best. Companies which deliberately hold back an individual for the company's good rather than the individual's more often than not come unstuck. Sooner or later the individual discovers that he or she is being exploited and then holds deep resentment against the employer, which surfaces either in performance at work or more likely in a decision to offer his or her services elsewhere. The basis of fair dealing with an individual is that the individual should know where he stands and the boss should understand the view point of the individual, what his ambitions and hopes are, and how a mutuality of interest can be developed between the him and the company.

It is easy enough to write about some of the difficulties of reward systems, but it is extraordinarily difficult to produce an ideal system. Moreover, pay systems tend to be the subject of fashions, partly because of the market pressures upon any pay system. At the present time we are seeing a heavy emphasis on performance related pay. This trend is partly due to an attempt to make pay a variable cost, so that the wages and salaries bill goes up only in accordance with the ability of the business to pay, and partly due to the belief that a substantially variable annual reward will prove a significant incentive for the individual. Despite the wholesale spread of performance-related reward systems, recent academic studies are once again casting doubt on their motivational effect. I have written elsewhere that my own experience corresponds much more closely to the teachings of Professor Herzburg. Many years ago Herzburg wrote that while 'unfair' pay is a demotivator, pay in itself is not a motivator. My early business days as a work study officer setting up and administering bonus schemes for people on the shop floor tended to confirm the truth of Herzburg's views.

There is nevertheless little doubt that performance-related pay systems do have the effect of channelling particular interests and concerns to specific aspects of the overall job – those which are likely to be rewarded. They will do so, however, at the expense of other aspects of the job and the formula which could unleash exactly the forces needed a year hence is very elusive. Moreover, as work becomes increasingly dependent upon the collaborative efforts of teams, individual performance-related pay systems may actually impede effective teamwork. Equally, a group per-formance-related pay system in which everybody receives the same percentage or bonus payment can barely be described as a motivator. Either of these two approaches lands one in trouble. A similar sum paid to everybody will appear generous to those at the bottom of the pile and hopelessly mean to those at the top. A percentage payment merely achieves a further increase in the usually already very wide gap between the payment of those at the top and those at the bottom. I am personally dubious about the validity of performance-related schemes because again, by definition, the performance related scheme has to apply to everybody. It therefore has to be capable of infinite gradation and consequently lands one yet again on the endless Tibetan prayer wheel of greater and greater complexity.

Payment systems are influenced, besides the problems of comparability and fashion, by a number of other factors. One of my only arguments with unions over a great many years has been their view that pay must be dealt with entirely on a group basis. Under this credo every fitter is entitled to the same pay regardless of whether he is good or bad at his job. It always used to amaze me that the very same shop steward who would argue endlessly that there was a rate for the job, which every man and women was entitled to, would none the less express horror if you chose X to do a particularly difficult aspect of the given job – saying 'For God's sake don't put X on to it, A is the only chap here who can do it.' When you then suggested that A was therefore entitled to a different payment from X you immediately fell foul of the basic credo of unionism in those days. Fortunately times move on, and union views with them. To pay everybody the same is as unfair as to have an infinite and necessarily somewhat arbitrary gradation of skills, where minute differences of pay tend to irritate rather than encourage.

The presence of elaborate mathematical pay systems provides a handy alibi for management. Managers like to be able to blame the system, or indeed anybody other than themselves, rather than accept their own inescapable responsibility for deciding and managing the rewards of their employees. The manager who is prepared to tell a subordinate that in his, the manager's opinion, the subordinate's work is worth X, no more and no less, and stand by that argument is a rarity indeed. While managers want to be able to produce an effect which corresponds to their own views and prejudices, they also inevitably like to be able to blame somebody else for those who are disappointed. Most managers' preferred pay system would give everybody a generous reward and a few people a super-generous one. Managers are just like every other human being, they want to be liked and admired by their people. They believe that people will work at their best if they believe they are constantly appreciated and rewarded. While in an ideal world everybody would respond only to kindness and appreciation, unfortunately very few can live on a diet of sugar alone. I have no doubt that the ratio of sugar to salt, carrot to stick, or praise to criticism should be weighed heavily in favour of the positive side. Nevertheless, constant reward without any form of criticism, striving for better performance or better results, or a constructive approach to higher effectiveness, produces a sloppy and de-tuned operation. Practically all of us work at our best when we are continuously being expected to achieve rather more than we think we can, but are rewarded and praised when we actually manage what we thought was impossible.

I return to Herzburg's statement that 'unfair' pay and

reward is a demotivator. It is amazing how happily people will work for long periods of time at rates of pay which they know to be somewhat less than the going rate, provided that the conditions, cause, and sense of solidarity is widespread. Under these circumstances pay and rewards are fair on an internal basis and are accepted as such, even though they appear to be below going commercial rates outside. You can expect a steady small leakage of people who will move on in order to earn the higher money, but it is incredible how many people will stay working contentedly within an organisation with whose aims they identify and where they believe that they are doing a really worthwhile job. If it were not for this fact virtually no charity could employ anybody in this country, for almost without exception charitable organisations cannot afford to pay rates competitive with, for example, stockbrokers. Nurses continue to nurse in the United Kingdom because they derive other satisfactions from their jobs besides the financial ones. Remarkably few people or organisations depend solely upon financial reward to keep and motivate their people.

Another factor which plays upon the whole question of reward systems is the concept of 'what we have, we hold'. Although I have reduced the pay of an individual on a very small number of occasions in my life, as a broad generalisation it is almost impossible to reduce pay without a totally disproportionate reaction. People are, however, prepared to have their pay frozen and eroded by inflation over a period of time. Certainly, where I have made a mistake and over-promoted a man and subsequently had to reduce him to a lower level, I have always taken a view that his pay had to remain frozen, because it had been my mistake in the first place to grant the promotion. The combined effect of all these factors is that pay tends to go only one way. It tends to move upwards continuously and to be ratchetted up both by the force of external competition and also by the methods which we use to administer pay systems within our companies. In my view many of the compensation consultants, with their systems and comparability, also add to the pressure upon this upward spiral.

Whilst I have homed in with a certain inexorability on financial pay systems, a little time must be taken out to consider that pay is only one part of the whole reward structure. It is important to look at rewards in the round. Rewards really encompass everything in business life, the organisation, hierarchical system, the opportunities for promotion, the opportunities for recognition, forms of recognition which may include titles, delegated authority, freedoms of action and control, and so on. Of course they encompass pay, but they have in the past also encompassed a ludicrously wide range of privileges: a different dining room, a different lavatory, a reserved car parking space and so on. The reward system also includes that indefinable and all too rare regulator of most of our lives, job satisfaction, which is a combination of the circumstances under which we work, the people we work for and our perception of the significance of whatever it is we are doing.

The reward system also embraces not only the values of the company but also its systems of punishment. Although

161

most companies go to great trouble to produce the most complicated reward systems, with numerous gradations of pay, privilege, status and so on, remarkably few go to any trouble at all to consider or outline the forms of punishment that may be exerted. Yet, as I pointed out earlier, the punishment side of the issue is equally as important as the reward. With no sanctions on behaviour or recognised ways of applying these sanctions no organisation will ever be kept tight and up to the mark. It is as important to express dissatisfaction as it is to express satisfaction. Moreover, most of us learn much more readily from the mistakes which are pointed out to us than from the successes we have achieved. A success achieved tends to encourage exactly the same solution and behaviour again, and this is all too seldom appropriate because of the rate of change in the environment in which we work. Whereas a pointed out and corrected mistake will definitely make one try to do something different the next time.

When looking at reward systems, therefore, the whole range of influencing factors have to be taken into consideration. Indeed, as the factors change, so the reward system itself has to be altered. Reward systems tend to be the subject of continual tinkering rather than reasonably frequent total reform. The tinkering invariably takes the form of introducing new elements and therefore reward systems tend to become more and more complex by a sort of natural process. Changes in the external world, together with changes in one's internal methods of organisation and one's expectations of people should, in my view, be more speedily reflected by changes in the total reward system. An example of this is the increasing trend towards flat non-hierarchical systems. I had believed for many years that the complexity of hierarchical systems have derived from the wish to use promotion as a form of reward in place of pay. The difficulty is that an ever increasing hierarchy makes the organisation sluggish, slow to respond and leads to all the business problems which we now so readily recognise. There is no doubt that job satisfaction within flat non-hierarchical organisations is much higher, as is the flexibility of the business. However, if you have a flat non-hierarchical system how do you reward and motivate the individual? How do you keep them striving for the pinnacle when you have actually removed the pinnacle – or at least many of the steps leading up to it? Will financial reward on its own provide the answer, or do you need some other acknowledgement of achievement to replace the happy experience of going home to tell your spouse at Christmas time that you have been promoted from assistant section manager to section manager? Unless the totality of the reward system is kept continuously in line with the aims of the business, one of the primary effects on the individual is vitiated and lost.

Reward systems tend to be set up for administrative convenience, and to assist budgeting and control. It is these pressures which lead to the established ritual of an annual pay award. Sadly, during practically all of my business life, an annual award has been a necessity, since I have always worked in inflationary conditions, which have meant that continuous adjustment of pay levels has been necessary –

even to keep people where they started. It is possible that the future may see a change in this arrangement, although I am one of those cynics who fails to believe that we are likely to find ourselves in a period of prolonged zero inflation, under which no salary changes will be necessary. Even within a zero inflationary environment reviews of salaries would still be required in order to acknowledge promotion and performance. Indeed, without progression in pay, sparked by productivity improvement, there is no way in which a country as a whole can get richer. There is an increasing wish on the part of most companies to link salaries more directly to the ability to pay and hence to the performance of the company as a whole. Every businessman or woman would love to have salary as a variable cost instead of a fixed one. Indeed every self-employed individual recognises that his or her salary is to some extent a variable cost, linked as it is directly to the ability of their business to generate the money to pay. Whilst the link between business success and the ability to pay is all too direct if you are, say, a self-employed plumber, it is very much more difficult to achieve in a company employing many thousands of people.

It is in order to achieve this more direct link that many companies are looking more carefully at profit sharing. My own experience of profit sharing, in a company which was one of the first to go this route in the United Kingdom, is that it speedily becomes absorbed into the pay package as a part of the total pay. When, under my chairmanship, it become necessary to cut profit sharing drastically – for the simple reason that there were no profits – the shock to our people was almost tangible. It could be argued that this demonstrated the effectiveness of the profit sharing system, and certainly an immediate feedback into the pay packet does bring the severity of the company's problems clearly and unmistakably to the attention of every employee. However, nearly every external financial pressure upon the company is not only to maintain the level of profits year in, year out, but to aim for a steady, predictable and inevitable increase in profitability every year. This gives a pleasing feeling that, in addition to the rest of the rewards, the profit sharing element itself will increase every year and most systems produce a sort of knock-on effect, so that the profit sharing element increases even more as a result of the increase in basic salaries, which are also contingent upon business success. The difficulty is that the whole effect is of a multiplier. Not only do wages and salaries increase proportionately faster, but the effect of a cutback tends to be limited to the reduction in profit sharing, rather than an actual reduction in salaries. None of these comments are meant to eradicate the belief that some form of involvement in the company by all the members of the company itself is a thoroughly good thing. However, my own strong preference is to have employee shareholders, rather than a financial allocation of profits. I believe those companies which have been set up with widespread employee shareholders, such as the National Freight Corporation, have demonstrated that the link, if large enough, can affect the operation of the company very strongly, particularly one which depends so self-evidently on the contribution of every man and woman for its ultimate competitiveness.

There is little doubt that in the United Kingdom there are very strong pressures for overt recognition of organisational success. Titles are of particular importance and almost everybody in the company seems to want to be described as a company director, hapless though that task may be. Certain terms in the United Kingdom are viewed as being derogatory. An American works manager is happy to be called a superintendent, but in Britain the title is viewed totally differently, even though the job may be the same. One reason why we give way to pressures for titles is the rather cynical view that titles do not cost anything – and therefore you do not mind what anybody is called. Unfortunately this is far from true. Easing off on the brakes on titles speedily leads to a proliferation of perceived ranks, each of which struggles to establish its place in the pecking order. A proliferation of titles tends to increase the rigidity of the organisation, and can lead speedily to the ridiculous view that 'it takes one to speak to one'. You therefore find that the contribution of somebody who is called section manager at a meeting which is attended by 'full' managers tends to be disregarded, even though he may be the best qualified person to speak on the subject. There is a disadvantage in avoiding the widespread use of titles. Pay differentials in the United Kingdom tend to be heavily skewed. At the lower levels of the industry they are extraordinarily small, whereas they stretch out speedily when you get to the top levels – almost on a logarithmic scale. Because of this most people wish to be able to demonstrate by means of the pecking order that they are making progress, or that they are at minimum well thought of. Other ways have to be found to meet this national requirement. It is perfectly possible to have a multiplicity of hierarchical ladders if this is the route that you consider to be most suitable for your business. You can have different grades of scientists, or marketing people, or of information technology specialists, although again great intellectual honesty is required to ensure that new ladders which are introduced do not bring with them a host of other business ills. At minimum there will be an expectation that a grading system of this type is linked in some recognisable way to rates of pay. Curiously enough, one of the areas where the effects of the pay system seems to me to be accepted most readily, despite its manifest imperfections, is the civil service. The system applied in the armed services and the one employed in many Japanese companies had several of the same features. Jobs were allocated to grades, and the only means of increasing one's pay was the speed with which one moved through the various grades. Within the grade there was also a continuing increase in payment for seniority and experience.

The system described could barely be further away from current practice in most businesses. It led to overlong hierarchies, it gave no direct reward for immediate effort, and it appeared to be an inflexible system which had barely altered over a great many years. It did however have one great virtue. The payment system was totally transparent and, in addition to this transparency, had the effect of channelling arguments about fairness entirely into the field of whether or not one should have been promoted. The fairness argument therefore honed in on the area where most people accept in any event that recognition and promotion will never be available for all and will always be affected by unquantifiable measures such as luck, your boss at the time, your particular suitability for the specific posting and so on. I certainly worked very happily within the service system for many years. The rewards of rank and promotion showed in a great many other ways besides the fairly modest increases in salaries that we obtained. Nevertheless, within the system of the Royal Navy there were considerable anomalies. The captain of the ship, any ship, no matter how small, received all sorts of honours, recognition and other forms of reward. Moreover, in my own service, the submarine service, it was perfectly possible to be the captain of a submarine at any rank from lieutenant to commander and at any age from early twenties to the forties.

These apparent anomalies brought me to the conclusion that a considerable degree of transparency about the system, accompanied by an openness about the results of the system would, in themselves, be good features of a proper reward system. Furthermore, I do not believe it is necessary to have a clear ascending system of pay which pervades from the very bottom to the very top of the company. I have on many occasions had people working for me who were paid more than I was. This has never worried me in the slightest, possibly because I believed that over a period of time my rate of reward would overtake theirs. But in any event, even when somebody of a lower perceived rank was paid more, I was still receiving the other rewards of the position of higher responsibility. I believe strongly that the details of any individual's pay are a private matter between the individual and the employer and the exact amount of money which is paid should not be public knowledge nor, as I have seen in some places, shown on a notice board. However, the system and principles under which payment arrangements are made should in my view be totally overt and clearly understood by all. They should be discussed, and where there are differences of opinion those opinions should be aired, although the views of the subordinates should not necessarily be adhered to.

The flip side of Herzburg, so to speak, which has been proven over and over again in almost every field of activity, is that what is perceived as unfair pay is a significant demotivator. 'Unfair pay' in fact becomes almost an obsession, dominates every other aspect of work and affects the whole relationship between the individual and the organisation. 'Unfair pay' is almost invariably related to relative rates of pay within one's own company, rather than the relationship between one's own business and the competition. People will still work perfectly well and happily in companies which are known as poor payers, provided there is belief and trust in the relative fairness of the reward system that pertains within the company. Employees know that dissatisfaction in that respect can always be met by choosing to move of one's own accord. It is of the greatest importance that managers should continuously be aware of the way in which the

169

reward and payment system is viewed. This is not to say that it is the duty and responsibility of the business to pay exactly what its employees want – or even in exactly the way which they would prefer. Nevertheless, acceptance of the principles under which pay is allocated, and support for it, is the critical factor in establishing the Herzburg definition of fairness. Just as it has always seemed to me foolish to apply an arbitrary shift system or hours of work without consulting one's people, so it seems to me that the involvement of one's people in the systems and the thinking behind one's payment systems is sensible, provided that the right to say no is clearly understood. It is better to have the debate in the open than to have a continual rumble of discontent going on in the background.

Ultimately the way in which a business or company rewards its employees has to be in tune with the values that the company espouses. A major gap between the professed values of the outfit and the way in which individuals are rewarded causes endless friction for very little net gain. After all, the reward system is meant to be a key enabler to help you recruit, motivate, and develop your people. It is not a minor part of the overall administrative system of the company, it is an absolutely crucial way in which the values and expectations of the company and its relationship with every individual it employs is expressed. It goes without saying that adhesion to the system is critical. Any diversion from what the company claims to be doing is absolutely fatal. There is always a suspicion on the part of employees that pay is a purely arbitrary system to enable the managers to indulge their particular favourites, and that their particular favourites are rewarded at least as much for their acceptability to the manager as they are for the attainment of the business goals. One of the many reasons why pay systems tend to be viewed with cynicism is because, as referred to in an earlier chapter, the theoretical organisation of the business and the way in which the business actually works are almost always at variance with each other. The prime individual driver and motor of a firm, although known to every member of the subordinate individuals and quite often recognised by the superiors, is nevertheless seldom recognised either hierarchically or in reward terms. Pay administration has to be punctilious and this is yet another reason to avoid the overriding complexity of most systems.

There are two particular aspects of rewarding which I believe are helpful, although they are all too seldom observed. The first is the importance of non-systematic immediate reward. This can take an infinite variety of forms, but the essence of non-systematic rewards is that they should happen as contemporaneously as possible with the action which merits the reward. The works management team who have just started up a plant and have been working sixteen to twenty hours per day, or without breaks for weekends, for three or four months, react overwhelmingly to an unscheduled week's leave to be taken immediately – even more so, of course, if they are actually handed the tickets and bookings for a holiday with their families. The immediate reward of a sum of money, from two hundred to a thousand pounds, accompanied by a meeting with and an expression of thanks from the manager for a job which had been outside the normal run of duty and has contributed visibly to the success of the business goals, has a much greater effect and is much less expensive than a salary increase at the end of the year, which will remain on the books for ever. Moreover, because the reward has not been budgeted for inside the family, it becomes a genuine reward. It enables something to be done for the whole family which nobody had expected and has, again, a totally disproportionate effect relative to the cost. I have referred many times to my own practice of sending a case of wine and thanks to any individual who seemed to me to have done something particularly meritorious. The essence of the reward is that it is a tangible way of saying thank you that is not put forward by the personnel department. Its form should be widely variable so that it does not, so to speak, come up with the rations, and it should be tailored to the particular needs or interests of the individual who is being rewarded. A bird watching holiday, a course of sailing lessons, a deep immersion French course in France are all ways of producing a truly memorable effect and saying thank you in a very public way at relatively low cost. What is required in all of these cases is a bit of thought. I believe that every manager should have a small 'float' to enable him to produce such forms of recognition in whatever seems the most appropriate way.

This is also an area where, if the performance justifies it, over-expenditure should not be leapt upon with hob-nailed boots. Recognition rewards are, after all, given after the task has been done and presumably the recognition means that the company has gained beyond what it expected. The exception, of course, is where you are rewarding somebody for having retrieved some unexpected or unscheduled disaster and reward in this case is equally important. Unscheduled rewards must be presented in ways which are public and overt. The fact that unscheduled rewards are made is in itself a message to all your people that you as a manager and the company as an organisation are interested in individuals and individual performance, that you are close to what is going on, that it is appreciated and that this appreciation can take a tangible form. In many organisations, such as local authorities, it is difficult to give substantial unscheduled rewards, but nothing stops you from giving recognition. When you are next making a public speech you can mention an outstanding job done by X or Y and thank the person publicly in front of others. Praise should always be given publicly, and admonitions should be given privately. One of the purposes of unscheduled rewards is to underscore public recognition in a way which passes a little bit of glory on to the individual who has won a reward. When praising, praise unstintingly – there is nothing worse than a grudging, penny pinching or ungenerous comment. Indeed, if you can not say something worthwhile or give something that will be appreciated do not do it at all. Just as it is perfectly possible to receive an ideal Christmas present which costs a relatively small amount of money but which is the result of real thought, and often takes the form of something which you had failed to realise you had needed or wanted, so it is with rewards. The art of the unscheduled reward lies in the

173

personalisation of the reward and the manner of its giving, as much as its cash value. I cannot be the only person who frequently attended retirement parties and was shocked at the apparent lack of consideration given to the presentation. A tiny silver bowl or a single candlestick seem a meagre reward for long years of devoted service.

The second area that I believe to be helpful, although again administratively difficult, is that of annual rewards. I believe there is a real advantage in giving the annual review of salary on a man or woman's birthday, rather than in one mighty bound at Christmas. While I realise that people worry about the aspects of control I believe there are good reasons for doing it this way. Of course, should the review be poor it is illusory to think that it is any easier to be nasty to somebody on their birthday than it is to be nasty to large numbers of people at Christmas. The fact is however that a birthday award is personalised and gives you time to spend with the individual, whereas if you are dealing with all your staff at Christmas it tends to be a matter of forming a queue outside the headmaster's study. A review at birthday time, or as near as one can get, also provides the opportunity of having an overall talk, not only about the performance last year, but about training and other needs, about areas of worry that the individual has and what can be done to improve his or her performance and so on. The money, or lack of it, therefore comes as a reinforcement of a general discussion of the individual, his ambitions, prospects and achievements. Moreover it makes it more difficult to make direct comparisons between individuals because the awards

174

are happening at different times. There is of course quite a bit more administrative work involved. If awards are being given in an inflationary situation it is necessary to know the annual inflation rate to the last date of the individual's award, but again such methods break down the uniformity of everybody getting three and a half per cent, or whatever it may be. I think the primary reason why there is such a reaction against annual birth date rewards is the difficulties which are then placed on budgeting for the year, but if we are indeed reaching a plateau of zero or very low inflation this particular problem will diminish markedly, because each year you will be working within a level of productivity improvement which you have to allocate across the piece.

In addition to unscheduled rewards and the timing of the annual review, I believe reward systems should put pressures on managers to award differentially. There are an infinite number of control systems which can achieve this result without an elaborate gradation system. A very simple ruling that, for every person paid about the average, there must be somebody paid below, forces a form of distribution. An even better one is to allocate a sum of money for bonuses or rewards, accompanied by an instruction that the minimum amount to be paid out of the kitty will represent an amount which forces distribution. For example, if the kitty is 10,000 for ten people, a rule that no amount paid may be less than 2000 will ensure some get nothing while others get a lot. All too many managers when given a bonus kitty to allocate will issue it absolutely equally to every member of their staff to avoid subsequent complaint – using the argument that it would be invidious to select any outstanding individual. Managers have to be encouraged to use freedoms in the reward system. They do not take to this approach naturally, nor do they enjoy the responsibility of administering rough justice. Equally it is important to look at the manager's performance in this area and discuss it with him when you have his appraisal and discuss his performance. A careful reading of the appraisals that he has given will show whether he is a consistently high or low marker but, even more to the point, will show whether he marks differentially at all. Large numbers of managers have found what they consider to be the simple way to the easy life by damning everybody with faint praise. Nobody is ever given a superlative write-up, but neither is anybody ever truly criticised. If that is the pattern of the managers behaviour it should be noted and drawn to his attention and his own reward system should be varied accordingly.

It is very easy to plot the distribution of rewards within a department and see whether they fall into any form of gaussian distribution, or whether the reward system is consistently slanted either towards generosity or meanness. Exact comparability and mathematical accuracy will never be achieved. A really effective manager will in fact actually have a greater number of good performers than the norm. In a department which is bowling merrily along you would expect to see higher levels of good performers than in a works or business which is performing in a lacklustre way. Perfect gaussian distributions are as suspect as reward or appraisal systems which have no variability within them at all, but there is no excuse for not knowing what the pattern is, and the way in which the pattern is applied says a great deal about the organisation, and even more about the managers concerned.

What therefore, in my opinion, would comprise the ideal considerations which are necessary for a decent reward system? I would hasten to say that I would hate to see the same reward systems applied everywhere. The most important three features of any reward system should be simplicity of the fundamental principles, singularity of the system and cohesiveness with the professed values and business behavioural characteristics of the company concerned. The reward system has to be supportive of the business objectives and operational aims of the company as a whole and its relationship has to be clear and visible. Within those broad parameters my ideal system would allow for very great individual flexibility – maybe even a payment system which I have seen being experimented with in a number of companies in the United Kingdom, a system where the individual can choose, within a wide range, the way in which the total amount of money which is to represent his remuneration can be delivered; flexibility between current salary, pension, car allowance or car, more or less holiday, etc. My ideal would also encourage the basic system to be supplemented by multiple recognition capabilities. There should be a wide variety of different ways in which exceptional work or contribution could be rewarded and recognised. These systems should not all be linked purely to numbers, but they must all be linked to specific achievement. The next characteristic

177

that I would wish to see would be that the system should force responsibility on managers for facing their obligations of levelling with their people, praising and rewarding the good, criticising and holding back the bad. In turn the manager's reward should be able to be affected by his willingness to undertake this most difficult of managerial tasks. Lastly, in my ideal, every individual should feel that his or her individual effort will be recognised, and that by their individual effort they can have some effect on the level of their financial rewards. It is all too easy to define what one would like to see, and all too difficult to achieve it. Nevertheless the importance of the reward system to the success of the company, and to the ability of the individuals within it to grow and prosper, is absolutely key. It is therefore worth spending a great deal of time thinking through what the company and the individuals within it are aiming for.

TEN Rejection

Although there is a plethora of books, management theories and studies of the systems of reward in business, the flipside, which is the subject of punishment and reproof, is barely touched upon. All management is a matter of balance. There should be a balance between encouragement and touches on the reins, and between rewards and reproofs. The way the curb is applied requires a least as much skill as the way encouragement is meted out. One of the curious things about business life is that, despite the fact that it is quite usual to give verbal encouragement, even gentle words of criticism are taken more deeply to heart than was intended. Many people in business are unaware of how their superiors view their performance and assume that they are performing worse than is the case. In the absence of indication of expectations or assessment of performance very few people have the self-confidence to believe lack of criticism is due to the excellence of their performance. By and large managers intensely dislike giving bad news. Like practically everybody else, they want to be liked and, unless they have got out of bed on the wrong side or have a vicious hangover, they are

179

not prone to criticise individuals to their faces. This does not of course prevent them slagging off both superiors and subordinates behind their backs.

When I left the Royal Navy and began work in business, I found the contrast in this area extraordinary. In the Navy there was little encouragement, you were seldom told that you had done a good job and, perhaps because of that, words of modest encouragement were valued. However, everyone, from your peers to your superiors at every level, was ready to criticise you and upbraid you mercilessly on any failure of performance – not infrequently in front of your subordinates. I used to long for a calm, imperturbable commander who would take me aside after a failure to explain what I had done wrong and why.

In business one often receives neither praise nor criticism. I spent my initial years in a state of constant concern that my performance was so appalling that my services were about to be dispensed with. Above everything, individuals need a degree of assurance about the perception of their performance and this seems to me a not unreasonable requirement. It is inevitable that most of us spend a lot of time considering how we are getting on; the first essential, therefore, is to have some yardstick of the performance expected, so that one can decide whether one is achieving what is required. It is helpful to have confidence that, if your performance is sub-standard, you will be told while there is still time to rectify the situation. So it is seldom that the absence of news is believed to represent good news. If an individual is indeed performing below expectation, it seems to me fair that the areas where they are failing should be indicated and they should be offered assistance to rectify the problem. The most detested organisations are those where there is barely a lift of the boss's eyebrows before, like a bolt out of the blue, one is told one's performance has been sub-standard for a long time and it has been decided to dispense with one's services.

In addition to the need for comments on the overall standards being achieved, there will always be a need for instant comment of a tactical kind. These comments tend to be about the minutiae of how the job is being done and come under the heading of friendly tips rather than statements of dissatisfaction. There is a big difference between the process of coaching and the process of reproof. Essentially, reproof is needed in two broad sets of circumstances. The first is when the individual has already been told not to do something – or to do something in a particular way – and, without reason or referral, has persistently refused to heed the advice or instruction. Once may be understandable but a repeat occurrence justifies a fierce rejoinder. The second area where reproof is necessary is more difficult. This is where the general overall performance of the individual is continually falling below expected standards. Sometimes it is sufficiently important to question whether it is in the interests of the individual and the company for them to continue to work together. It may be possible for the individual to correct these failures, in which case it is vital to ensure that he or she is given clear guidance to give him every chance to get back on course. If the failure cannot be corrected, it is in

181

everyone's interests for a parting of the ways to occur. That a person has failed to come up to your expectations does not mean he or she will fail everywhere; it may be a simple mismatch, or that their skills and strengths lie in areas you have not used. Continual failure destroys self-belief until so little confidence is left that a man or woman becomes flotsam on the seas of life. It is all the more important, therefore, that individuals should not waste time in finding their particular niche and role.

When people are performing below par a dressing-down session will often reveal extraneous and unexpected items which may explain poor performance. Few people perform less well over time, though they may perform less assiduously as they become familiar with the tasks they have been set. In particular, one should always be careful to ask probing questions when a good performer goes off the boil. If there is a major change in performance, it is almost always due to some extraneous factor, and it is up to the boss to find out what that may be. There is another circumstance where a genuine mistake is made by both parties. The individual may not be what you first thought he was, he may not fit in, his position in the team may not have worked out, or his levels of skills or personal qualities may not be adequate. Reproof in this circumstance is a preparatory step towards the big farewell; it is a waste of time to try to influence matters which the individual cannot change. Drawing attention to weaknesses which are inherent and incapable of alteration simply reduces self-esteem and can speedily drive

182

you and the individual into a spiral of mutual distrust and incapacity to perform.

The level of aspiration and the speed of performance and delivery you expected of subordinates is always set by the manager. The careful manager will consistently set the level of aspiration higher than the individual believes he or she can achieve, but it should be possible with a little coaching and pushing. As I have already pointed out this is a precise calculation and the manager may get it wrong; it is therefore important to be clear whose fault a failure in performance is. The manager may have set his sights beyond the capability of even the most outstanding subordinate to perform or, more frequently, the level of aspiration may be okay but requirements for the speed of achievement are beyond the capacity of even the speediest employee. The best performers believe that ultimately they will reach a stage where nothing more is required of them and they can coast and enjoy the fruits of success, so it is essential to keep pushing for more. It is, however, equally essential to praise success, particularly when there have been unexpected levels of achievement. Not infrequently the boss and the subordinate are equally surprised that something has come off; if this happens, it is a good idea to have a joint celebration.

Managers have to be clear that taking risks is not a natural habit for most people; women in particular are almost bio-logically conditioned to avoid it. With the exception of the few who are born gamblers, most people try to avoid or to minimise risk. Most mistakes are made by people taking risks in ignorance, rather than calculated risks which fail to come off. When individuals take calculated risks, it is inevitable that mistakes will be made. While some reproof may be necessary, there must be a balance between jumping on the individual with such force that they will never again take another risk and encouraging the risk-taking but pointing out the reasons underlying the failure.

Risk-takers who fail blame themselves excessively. In business failure is always public and it is unlikely that a mistake can be concealed for any length of time. My favourite example of this is the salesperson who loses a sale. The paradox is that unless the salesperson is willing to risk losing the sale they will not get the best price, but at some point they will fail and the sale will be lost. The failure is public and everybody is aware of it. The paradox is that when the salesperson gets the sale time after time he or she is viewed as merely doing the job – what are salespeople for except to sell? Unfortunately, they not only have to sell but they have to do so at the best possible price; the easiest way to achieve the former is to abandon the pursuit of the latter. In reality the salesperson who from time to time loses a sale, provided he has done so through trying for the highest price, requires encouragement rather than reproof.

It is of the greatest importance that the manager should understand what is involved when criticising his subordinate. He must be clear what he is trying to achieve by the criticism and he needs to understand the events that have led to the need for criticism. It is often worthwhile sitting down with the subordinate and starting by having a lengthy chat about what happened and what they feel were the circumstances which led to the failure or mistake. This will establish your credentials for fairness, and mean that any consequent discussion or criticism is based on the same interpretation of the facts. Most employees have an understandable wish to deflect criticism on the basis that the manager did not understand what had happened. Better by far to establish some common ground and perception so that this escape route is blocked. Although criticism should never be made in anger and certainly never in public, it is always best applied as soon as possible after the mistake has occurred. If there is a long delay, the individual tends to cocoon a mistake in a protective carapace which places a lot of the responsibility everywhere except on themselves.

The trick is to take a little while to reflect about the mistakes made and whether a critical discussion will help or not, and then to decide the objectives of the discussion. Plainly, one of the main objectives will be to prevent the mistake happening again, not to produce a grovelling apology from a chastened subordinate. The reality of life is that people seldom make exactly the same mistake twice. Most, provided they have mentally acknowledged that something has gone wrong, will be watching that particular area with great intensity. However, this means that they will probably make their next mistake in an associated area, because of their concentration on preventing a repetition of the first error. If the mistakes are ones the individual can correct himself or herself, it is better to limit your criticism to comments such as, 'That didn't go very well, did it?'or 'Oh dear', rather than have a full-blown court martial and commission

185

of enquiry. It may be, however, that the mistake is one of a series or suggests some underlying trend worth nipping in the bud.

Over-optimism and a tendency not to bear the downside in mind sufficiently strongly when taking a view of the future are trends worth following up quickly, rather than waiting for further developments. If this is the case, you must point out the three or four examples which have led you to suspect what you are trying to correct. If the problem is over-optimism, you need only a fairly minor adjustment, because the best creative managers always have an unshakeable belief that things will go right – albeit with a good deal of help on their part – and you do not want them to go from full ahead to full astern in one quick move.

The keys to criticism and reprimand lie above all in consistency coupled with integrity, fairness and, as near as possible, transparency. It is difficult to generate trust when critisising, but there is no time in relationships between individuals where trust is subjected to greater trial and where its existence is more essential for achievement of the aim. In this search for consistency the annual appraisal plays a particularly important role, and it is vital that the manager is both the appraiser and the appraised. A well-carried-out appraisal and interview should tell you as much about yourself and your abilities as a manager as it does about the person appraised. Although appraised and appraiser are inevitably more influenced by contemporaneous events, the discussion is meant to cover the entire year of work. When things are going well this is relatively easy, but when things are going badly it becomes a more difficult operation.

If performance is below the expected level nine out of ten individuals are aware of this and are already worried, particularly if the balance between approval and criticism has tilted too far. Only the super-confident employee actually looks forward to appraisal, and on occasions may need taking down a peg or two. If both you and the appraised feel that things have not been going as well as they should, it is probably sensible to start probing into the employee's personal background. Worries about health, finance and family problems have a direct effect upon performance; the mere sharing of these concerns may help, and it is always possible that you may be able to help. Perhaps you can get a second medical opinion, or arrange a loan or an advance on pay. Even if it is not possible for you to do anything to relieve these concerns, it is helpful to know whether performance is being affected by external factors, and it is reasonable to suppose that these worries will not last for ever and that the standard of work will improve.

If there do not appear to be any personal extraneous circumstances which are affecting the employee's performance the next thing to do is to check that the failure is not your own. You may have set the hurdles too high, perhaps made inadequate allowance for lack of experience, or you may not have delegated the necessary authority to perform. It is important to be as probing and honest about your part in the failure as you are about theirs. Is it basically lack of effort or is it one of intrinsic incapability? If you feel that

187

you are asking more than the individual is capable of, even after additional coaching, you have to consider whether a change in his or her role within the company may not be in both your best interests. Companies and individuals only perform well when there is a mutuality of interest and advantage to both.

Over-promoting someone is a not uncommon fault and it would be grotesque to place the blame for that on the individual. If someone has been over-promoted the worst thing is to try to prop them up by bringing in a super-efficient subordinate to carry the load. This is unfair to the subordinate and further destroys the self-esteem and peer perception of the individual. You do not resolve a problem where you have been unfair to one party by being unfair to another. Equally it is unjust to fire someone who has been over-promoted because of your misjudgement. A sideways or downward move may well be the best action to take. The fact is that if someone is failing in their job he or she are usually as aware of this as you are. If they are doing everything they can and the fault is one of expectation, there is frequently a feeling of relief when they are relieved of that particular responsibility. But it is very important that they are given a real job, and one they can actually perform. Finding a parking place to carry an over-promoted executive is destructive to the company and to the individual. The person soon knows that he or she is the recipient of kindness, and their self-esteem takes yet another knock.

In my early days as a manager I over-promoted an excellent buyer and made him into a section manager. By contrast

188

with his clarity and decisiveness about buying decisions, he was a failure when asked to guide and direct the efforts of others. Despite its being viewed as an unconventional response, I grasped the nettle and moved him back to being a buyer, albeit in a different part of the department. However, I ensured that he kept the additional salary he had been awarded on promotion until, with the passing of time and effects of inflation, the salary for his new position caught up. I was straightforward with him and accepted the blame for the mistake; I also told him that I could ill afford to lose his buying capabilities. The whole question resolved itself very well – not only did the section return to full power but he was even more determined to demonstrate to me and to his colleagues what an excellent buyer he was.

One of the important responsibilities of a manager is to preserve the self-esteem of the subordinate, and even more so if the subordinate is likely to have to leave the company at some stage. It is bad enough to lose your livelihood without simultaneously losing your belief in your ability to earn a living. There cannot be a worse advertisement for your management than a string of people who leave your employment as wounded individuals, and you have to carry a particularly large layer of responsibility for this. People are never neutral after being fired, every man or woman who leaves your company will speak either for the company or against it. The problem is made worse because each of us hates discharging someone, particularly someone you have tried to work with for a fair period of time. There is an inevitable tendency to justify your actions by demonstrating, to the individual and to the outside world, that you have acted fairly and that the person is useless and incapable of doing a proper job. This must be strenuously resisted. After all, you still have your job and your pay packet is still coming in; the other person is leaving for your convenience and because you believe that you and the company will be better without them. Generosity of spirit and concern should be the order of the day: thinking carefully about the individual's strengths and helping him to find a job where he can prosper, instead of taking one where they may fail again. It is to your advantage if, after leaving you, they do succeed. They will remember the help you gave and will look upon the actions you took as being fair and, in the long term, in their interests.

As I have said, one of the greatest traps when discharging an individual is the urge to justify your actions and to have the person tell you how fair and decent you have been. No one ever thinks redundancy will happen to them, so no matter how carefully the interview is carried out, the individual almost always goes into a state of shock and finds it difficult to pay attention to your words and evasions. All the employee remembers is that they have been fired and their minds are filled with the horrors of facing their family and friends and their fear of the future. They probably feel that it is unfair, and are certainly not thinking about your feelings – after all, you are still employed. Time is needed for them to adjust before any rational discussion can take place.

The first session is, in my experience, best conducted along

190

the lines of 'I am afraid we have to reduce our costs and numbers if the company is to survive. I have had to choose who goes and I have reluctantly decided that you must be one of them. Blame me for this decision – it does not reflect on your abilities or efforts, and I am certain we can find you a new career elsewhere. Because of my responsibility for this decision, I intend to do everything possible to help you. There is no hurry about leaving. You will want to think about this and discuss it with your family first but I would like to sit down with you soon to discuss where we go from here.' I have no time for the formula of clearing desks and leaving immediately. If handled correctly the employee will continue to do his or her job well, if only to show you and colleagues how wrong the decision is. The next discussion will probably require a good deal of time. It is best to start by discussing the redundancy terms being offered; obviously the more generous these can be the better. Because of the speed of changes affecting business, changes of job are a permanent part of the scene, and if your company is to attract good people, it will need a reputation for decency and fair treatment of those who have to go.

Unfortunately the shock of losing a job makes it difficult for people to think of further changes; most want to find another exactly like the one they have just lost. Their pride and their financial circumstances make it difficult for them to contemplate a lower-status job with lower pay, even though it may offer the best prospects in the long term. They will not be facing this situation often and it is important to try to focus on the future. As well as being an unwelcome

191

shock, redundancy can be an opportunity to start again and refocus. It can be an opportunity to rethink and to take into account the range of hobbies, interests, places to live and so on which have been the stuff of dreams in the past. People need a lot of help if they are to turn the chance they did not want into an opportunity to enhance their lives. Many firms use outplacement counsellors and specialists to help in this process, and they can certainly contribute provided they are not used as a means of passing on your problem. If you have made someone redundant, it is your responsibility to help them. This responsibility cannot be dumped on the personnel department, the outplacement consultant or the labour exchange. You have removed the certainties from an individual's life and your personal support and help is the least you can provide in return.

Surprisingly few people who are made redundant think of setting up their own business, perhaps because the redundancy removes some of their confidence. Sometimes you can help to set up former employees as suppliers or subcontractors to your business, and the possession of an ongoing contract, even for a year or two, is often enough to launch people on their own. Above everything, the redundant employee needs to feel that he or she has not been abandoned, and it can be helpful to have someone in the background – looking at the books, helping with introductions, assisting with retraining to follow a new career, meeting for lunch or dinner every few weeks. These small interventions can make the difference between future success and failure.

Nothing blunts the initial shock of being made redundant, but good managers will be surrounded by people who tell them that being made redundant was the best thing that ever happened to them. There is no single area where the conductor of the orchestra has more responsibility than to ensure that the players who leave live to play again.

ELEVEN 'Requiem'

During my thirty-eight years in industry I have seen unbeliev-able changes in attitudes towards the management of people, and in the whole role and theory of motivation, leadership and teamwork. I joined ICI at the height of the period of enlightened paternalism. The best companies had a deep concern for their people, but this concern took the form of total belief that the company and its leaders knew what was the right thing for every man and woman who worked for them. The company sought to supply a total life for every-body, football teams, sports and recreation clubs and every other sort of activity. Even as the grateful recipient of this attention and largesse, I remember being concerned that I was too dependent on my employer and lessened as an individual by so being.

I had come from the Navy where the attitude to those serving was that they belonged to the Services lock, stock and barrel. The Navy believed and acted as though it had complete command over every moment of your life and aspect of your activities. You were not allowed to get mar-ried without permission and the Navy graciously told you when you were old enough to do so. Leave or holidays were considered a privilege and nobody was ever entitled to time off. I found that the mere act of joining the Royal Naval College at the age of thirteen had committed me to serve as long as the Royal Navy wanted me. The flip side of this awesome list of expectations was that the Navy sought to look after every aspect of your life. When I worked in Germany, every facility was provided, even my groceries. It is not perhaps surprising that when I left such a restrictive life I felt ill equipped to cope with the complexities of life on my own. I had become reliant on my monthly pay cheque which though it was inadequate and seldom increased, there was no likelihood that it would be reduced.

When I faced the necessity of supporting my wife and child in the weird and alien world of business I was therefore relieved to find that there were companies who took a similarly broad view of their responsibilities. Indeed, when I was recruited into ICI I was assured that I had a job for life. There is not the remotest possibility that someone joining a company in the 1990s will be given such a comforting message and, indeed, not many would even want to feel they had committed themselves so wholeheartedly at such an early stage.

These paternalistic attitudes, although comfortable in some ways, led to a reduction in the wish to steer one's own course and, equally easily and perhaps inexorably, led to an increase in the power of the unions, acting on behalf of groups of people rather than of the individual. Allowances for the individual showed themselves in the welfare aspects of the paternalistic approach. My employer was concerned if any member of my family was unwell and when I joined ICI I received help and advice regarding my daughter's treatment, introductions to specialists in the area and continued concern about her welfare and well-being. These patterns of behaviour had been a reaction against the historic approach where labour was a unit of production and hired by the hour to do a specific task. Indeed, dealing with people this way still existed at that time in the docks and certain other industries. Although enlightened firms had tried to build up relationships with their staff, they were those of master and servant rather than of fellow members of a team. Even without the vast changes in technology and the organisation of work that were taking place it was inevitable that these attitudes would change. They appeared appropriate and consistent at a time when people were hired for a mixture of their physical and mental abilities. In many cases the mental involvement was minor and the practised operator could speedily get into a routine where performance of his tasks was almost second nature, rather as driving a car seldom occupies the individual's total attention. Meanwhile, their minds ranged across the breadth of their outside interests and they derived many of their satisfactions from the hobbies they pursued outside their workplace.

These attitudes to management were changing fast by the beginning of the eighties, when the political attack on corporatism in the United Kingdom really took place. For a short time the extremes of paternalism appeared to be replaced by a philosophy that almost amounted to 'every man for themselves'. There were massive and politically inspired reductions in the power and privileges of the unions, and the restraining influence the unions had on poor management was markedly reduced. Management was handed back 'the power to manage' which they themselves had walked away from in the days of extreme union power. I do not believe that we had ever lost the power to manage; it had just become more difficult and required more skill and determination. Those managers who claimed that they were prevented from running their businesses by union power had, in many cases, simply abrogated their wish to control its destiny. The doctrine that there was 'no such thing as society' and that every man's and woman's responsibility was to do the best they could for themselves appeared to me as antipathetic to the pursuit of effective management as the extremes of paternalism and union power had been in their day. Economic factors have an ugly and inevitable way of forcing uncomfortable realities upon us and it is difficult to buck an economic trend indefinitely. But, as I had learnt in my early days as a work study officer, financial factors on their own do not lead to inspiration or happiness, or to the commitment and assumption of responsibilities and tasks essential for business success.

This trend towards individuals taking sole responsibility for themselves was accompanied by a number of other predictable changes. People began a merry-go-round of business moves because by so doing they believed they could better themselves more quickly than by staying with a single employer. They viewed the attractiveness of jobs in terms of pay and perquisites rather than that elusive and derided factor 'job satisfaction'. Without question, individuals had needed to be encouraged to take more responsibility for themselves and their futures, but few had been given any preparation, training or understanding of what was involved. Moreover, it is extraordinarily difficult to manage one's own development, and often without help or input from anybody else. Under the force of economic pressure, organisations realised that it was no longer possible to produce a career from cradle to grave for their employees.

Meanwhile, changes in technology and the force and speed of international competition led to a multiplicity of experiments and changes in organisations and ways of working. There was widespread recognition that economic forces alone made it impossible to run organisations with long management hierarchies and determined efforts were made to reduce costs to competitive levels to force more and more responsibility down the line, reducing the numbers of supervisors and the cost of overheads. Working in these ways involved entirely different concepts of the relationship between the managed and the managers and of shared responsibility, both for the task and for the individual's growth, welfare and development. Although these concepts followed from competitive pressures, the change in the balance of power between the individual and the organisation delayed the recognition of the different management skills required. In too many cases management paid less and less attention to the individual, believing that if they managed the 'hard' economic factors it was up to the individuals to adjust. If they would not or could not do so, it would be easy enough to find others who would.

Sharing responsibility is possible in practical terms only when all parties accept that they are interdependent and, as interdependent beings, do not have complete power over the other. There appeared to me to be a management backlash in a number of places where, feeling that they had been run ragged by their workforce and the unions for many years, management seized the changes in the balance of power in terms of 'now it is your turn to do as we tell you'. There are still a number of organisations and companies who have built up a legacy of foolish and ill-considered misuse of power, which will have to be overcome before they can work constructively with their people.

When the recession at the end of the eighties proved both deeper and more protracted than anybody expected, the confidence that there would always be a job for those willing to work evaporated very quickly. At the same time, the only way out of their problems that many managers could see was reducing costs and, inevitably and invariably, reducing the numbers of employees. Indeed, in a recessionary situation the wages and salaries bill and a cessation of new investment are the first factors to take the strain. Day after day the newspapers and the media were full of announcements of massive reductions in manning. In their newfound belief in a world where individuals had to look after themselves against a background of increasing opportunity, people had borrowed injudiciously and had invested in mortgages and housing in the belief that their personal circumstances could only continue to improve. This in turn made security of employment even more essential when it was becoming more difficult to obtain.

The whole period was accompanied by changes in the role and expectations of personnel management. In the days of paternalism the personnel director had been a combination of welfare officer and a specialist in the arcane complexities of union negotiation. People who had entered the personnel field had done so because they wanted to 'work with and help people'. It was a time when sociology departments in universities blossomed, and where personnel was viewed as 'being nice to everybody'. During the eighties the role changed abruptly. Personnel departments and personnel managers were given an altogether harder edge. They were expected to become experts at demanning, closing down factories, relocating and retraining and redundancy. Although these tasks were seen as being directly related to business objectives and business survival the personnel people were still seen as specialists ensuring that the necessary changes were made with the minimum of disruption and maximum cost effectiveness. Fortunately, memories of paternalism and welfare meant that many people were concerned to carry out the massive adjustments required in as humane and involved a way as possible. However, as the decade wore on, redundancies, firings and changes of course were increasingly seen as a natural part of business life to which the individual should be accustomed and should adjust. The difficulty is that, as I know from friends of mine who have been made redundant on more than one occasion, familiarity does not make the adjustment any easier. Indeed when, through no fault of your own, you have been made redundant two or three times it almost impossible to retain any self-confidence and one can only admire the willingness of such people to pick themselves up and fight anew.

The world of work has become an increasingly lonely place. It may be that we were put here to learn individual responsibility and how to look after ourselves, but these are extraordinarily difficult things to manage without outside assistance. Everyone needs a mentor or coach. Even chairmen of large companies need input from their peers and subordinates and, ideally, a close friend, if they are to develop their skills and abilities, and clarity about one's limitations as well as one's abilities is the rarest of human gifts. Moreover, even if one had an accurate perception of one's limitations, it is impossible to know how one is viewed by others – an essential ingredient in building a team or relationships with groups of people.

And so we come to today, facing a further decade of change and ever fiercer international competition from peoples with different histories and expectations to our own.

I believe strongly that, both for individuals and for companies, the future lies in recognition of the interdependence of the company or group and the individual, and the development of skills and concepts which will enable that interdependence and relationship to be enhanced and improved. This is a very different form of management from that in which most of us have been brought up. It calls for sensitivity, wisdom, openness of mind, ability to listen and to trust, and it requires decency of a demanding type. A friend recently challenged my view that it was possible to manage people while still being a nice person. I replied that it had to be possible; it is simply not credible that only the selfish, insensitive, rash and brash can create and lead teams. Teams can work together only if they trust, and trust requires mutuality of respect, integrity, and mutuality of regard. These are not attributes one normally finds amongst the villains of this world, and they do not sit easily with personal ambition. Plainly, every business manager and leader is not (nor could we expect them to be) a saintly person. Nevertheless, unless management and leadership involve decent virtues and the fair use of power, it is unlikely that groups of people will operate at their best.

I started this book by pointing out that competition for the future lay more and more between the commitment and brain power of groups of people of different nationalities in a struggle for competitive success which is constantly getting tougher and is never-ending. Business in the nineties is, even more than in the past, a marathon relay. Being in front merely gives one the right to try harder. It means that you are setting the pace which every competitor has to beat. Continuing success for you and your team involves maintaining a faster pace than those behind you can hope to overtake, and this cannot be done by the enforced will power of a single person. It is the team working together, feeling responsibility for each other, understanding clearly that one has constantly to improve his or her own performance and that of those around them, which enables the race to be won.

We are going to see further big changes in the ways in which people are managed. I do not believe anyone today thinks that the management of people is just a matter of welfare, or that it can be left, as a speciality job, to the personnel department and the personnel director. The management of people is the task of the managers of the enterprise, whatever it may be: a hospital, a school, a regiment or a ship, a manufacturing factory, or an office. If we and our businesses are to succeed it will be because we have a greater understanding of the forces at work and are prepared to make a marked change and improvement in the standards of skill and attention to the care, leadership and development of all our people. I am indeed conscious that much of the experience which this book draws on is already out of date. Even though I remain involved in the business world, this unusual angle enables me to take a different perspective. When involved in the day-to-day battle for survival, it is notoriously difficult to stand back and examine honestly and creatively the forces at work. It is in the hope that these perspectives may help my friends and colleagues who are directly involved in the battle of managing in an ever tougher external environment that this book has been written.

As I said in the beginning, if our country is to survive and prosper, it can do so only by utilising to the full the latent abilities and talents of all our people, and it is the task of the managers to make that happen. On their success must

204

depend many of the hopes and ambitions we share for a better tomorrow. It is the conductor of the orchestra who creates the magic of a group of free and individual talents working in harmony to produce ever better and more memorable music.

Index

Index

Index